UNSUPER MOMMY

Release expectations, embrace imperfection, and connect to God's superpower

Maggie Combs

BroadStreet
PUBLISHING

BroadStreet Publishing Group, LLC
Racine, Wisconsin, USA
BroadStreetPublishing.com

UNSUPERMOMMY: Release Expectations, Embrace Imperfection, and Connect to God's Superpower

ISBN-13: 978-1-4245-5411-9 (hardcover)
ISBN-13: 978-1-4245-5412-6 (e-book)

Stock or custom editions of BroadStreet Publishing titles may be purchased in bulk for educational, business, ministry, fundraising, or sales promotional use. For information, please e-mail info@broadstreetpublishing.com

Cover design by Chris Garborg at www.garborgdesign.com
Typesetting by Katherine Lloyd at www.theDESKonline.com

Printed in China

17 18 19 20 21 5 4 3 2 1

To my husband, Wes,
who always believed this was
God's plan for me.

Contents

Embracing Imperfection: Step 1-Give Up on Measuring Up

Have you ever met a supermommy? Her baby sleeps soundly, nurses happily, and meets every milestone ahead of schedule. She tosses her perfectly wavy hair over her shoulder as she tidies her already sparkling house with nontoxic, organic soaps while her sweet cherub plays quietly with a wooden teether on a knit blanket on the floor. Naptime is just long enough for her favorite hobby and a spunky exercise routine. Her doting husband arrives home in time to kiss her cheek and pinch her baby-weight-free behind before playing with the baby while she creates a healthy and delicious dinner.

If we're honest, we all want some of that supermommy life. Unfortunately, it's a fantasy. It's time to be transparent about our real lives and give up on measuring up to supermommy standards. Trust me, embracing an imperfect life as an unsupermommy serving a super-powerful God is joyful freedom.

This book won't instruct you how to do motherhood perfectly. I won't tell you how to raise your child, but I will push you to let God change your heart. You'll discover how the gospel offers redeemed imperfection and more of God even if you're failing by the world's standards. If you're pregnant, your heart is full of lovely desires for how your motherhood will look and the kind of home your child will experience, but if you're already a mom, you probably know the brutal truth: motherhood often feels like failure upon failure.

The world around us is filled with bloated expectations for moms. Even though logically you probably know that no one can live up to those standards, it's nearly impossible not to internalize them. These standards aren't all bad on their own. It's the assumption beneath the standards—that we can control our circumstances—that's fatal to our joy.

But there is hope! You may not have the ability to succeed at the expectations piling up at your feet, but God's strength is mighty in your weakness. He has more than enough power to connect to when you discover that you just aren't strong enough. Ultimately God's goal is not to enable supermommies, but to develop us into women whose humble hearts earnestly love and desire more of him.

I'm a fairly new mom myself. I had my first baby five years ago. Then I had two more, for a total of three boys in just shy of three years. Only God could orchestrate such chaos. With the first two boys, I experienced not infertility but delay in getting pregnant. We *knew* we didn't get pregnant easily. We were wrong. My second son was only five months old when I took a pregnancy test on a whim after some morning queasiness. I needed to put my mind at ease. So much for that!

I've had three newborn baby experiences in quick succession. I'm not reminiscing fondly from ten years down the road; instead, I'm soldiering through the endless loads of laundry, a constantly messy kitchen, showerless days, and sleepless nights right along with you. I don't have this all figured out. God is teaching me his truth as I write. I'm not a perfect mom, and I'm not an expert, but I have to speak this word: Dear Mommy, don't live in shame for being pushed beyond your limits. You can break free from unnecessary expectations and embrace imperfections covered by God's superpower.

Here's What You Don't Know

My dad loves to remind me, "You don't know what you don't know." Let me tell you, I had no idea what I didn't know about the spiritual impact of being a mommy. When I was pregnant, everyone told me the first year would be rough, but no one explained why. Now that I have done it three times, I'm starting to figure it out. The problem with motherhood is that you're starting from scratch with everything. I didn't know the first thing about taking care of a baby. I had a major learning curve there. Even if I had been a baby person (I'm not) or a full-time nanny for ten years (I wasn't), I would have been completely unprepared for the real trial: identifying the good desires of motherhood that are usurping the best desire—knowing, loving, and glorifying God.

With the birth of her baby, a mother also births an entirely new set of desires for her life. Some of these new desires come from the lengthy set of expectations our society has for mothers. A pregnant woman is inundated with expectations from her doctor, fellow moms, friends, parents, blogs, baby websites, social media groups, and pregnancy books. She develops a master plan for motherhood, full of the grandiose expectations she has willingly (or sometimes at the insistence of others) adopted to fashion the best life for her baby. It's more than a birth plan; it's a life plan, and it feels awesome and untouchable.

Then baby comes and one or all of her plans don't work out. Now mommy feels like a failure. Of course, she's not really a failure! She's just a real-life imperfect woman, with a unique child, whose perfect plan needs to be adapted to meet their combined needs. The real trial stems from her reaction to her circumstances; when a mom lets her expectations become more important than God's plan, her good desires can develop into something ugly.

God explains it best in James 1:13–15: Let no one say when he is tempted, "I am being tempted by God," for

God cannot be tempted with evil, and he himself tempts no one. But each person is tempted when he is lured and enticed by his own desire. Then desire when it has conceived gives birth to sin, and sin when it is fully grown brings forth death.

James explains that we can't blame God or Satan for our temptations; they stem from our desires. God doesn't say "evil desires," which means even our good desires can trip us up. Desire gives *birth* to sin—oh, how appropriate for mothers. We have so many desires—for ourselves, our children, our husbands—and they're *good* desires!

The problem is allowing our good desires to reign unchecked by our desire for God. A good desire starts so small that you can't even feel it growing inside of you. As that desire grows, it starts kicking against everything around it. Eventually you can't think about anything else anymore. Everything you do is impaired by it. Sound familiar, pregnant mommies? Unchecked desires become expectations, and expectations become wants, and wants become needs. When something we feel we *need* goes unmet, we sin to get it.

Sin doesn't feel justifiable for a simple desire, but a *need* deserves drastic measures. This is the conundrum of the Christian life: we can never completely escape the growth of our desires into needs. Paul David Tripp calls the word *need* "the sloppiest, most all-inclusive word in the human language."[1] There's an endless list of *needs* for our babies, our husbands, and ourselves when we allow our desires to become more important than God's plan for us.

The hardship of motherhood isn't our strenuous circumstances; it's our stubborn hearts. Before motherhood, I knew what my normal sin patterns were: worry, need for the attention and approval of others, and pride, just to name a few. Despite these sin patterns, I had always been capable to perform any job given me in my own power. Then I underwent the colossal lifestyle modification of wife to mother, shifting my desires and revealing new sin patterns. For the first time in my life, I wasn't able to meet simple expectations, and I fought endless emotional battles to win back the feeling of being capable and productive. No matter how hard I worked, I couldn't manage to measure up to either the world's standards for moms or my own standards for how I thought motherhood should go.

Unfortunately, this didn't lead to victory but to discarding the one thing I truly needed: more of God. The hardest part of becoming a mom isn't the loss of sleep or crazy hormones; it's the raging unchecked desires for our new lives overtaking our desire for God. It's the grasping, endless pursuit of the unreachable goals for our babies, ourselves, and our husbands.

We know the problem. Now we must search out solutions.

This book outlines specific, good desires for your baby,

yourself, and your husband. We'll walk together through unplugging from some common expectations in motherhood that are commandeering the throne of our heart. We are weak and fallen. We will never be perfect moms. We will fail every day. **But he gives more grace** (James 4:6).

God is grace and mercy, perfect love, and complete rightness. When we get mothering wrong, God gets everything right. His power is stronger than all our weakness. God's grace is sufficient for our tasks, redeeming of our failings, transforming of our attitudes, and abundant enough to always surpass our expectations. God's grace is always greater than our imperfections. It's time for us to give up on measuring up and fall into the faithfulness of our super-powered God.

This book will also walk you through four steps of fully embracing your imperfection as a means to God's super-power. We're already working on Step 1 right now: Give Up on Measuring Up. God doesn't want our self-made super-mommy. He wants to use our failures to give us more of him: **For when I am weak, then I am strong** (2 Corinthians 12:10). Let's embrace our weakness as the ticket to God displaying his strength in our lives. Let's release the control of raising our children into the hands of the One who loves them infinitely more than we do. Then we can move forward in our imperfection, expecting God's super-powered grace to redeem it for his glory.

Let's begin with believing the gospel: Jesus came to sacrifice himself for all our sins and imperfections. The grace offered to us on the cross is all we truly *need* for this life. When our hearts are filled with his unending goodness to us first, we don't need to grasp at our expectations. If God is sufficiently big in our lives, we no longer worry about measuring up.

Jesus measured up for us on the cross. If we keep the throne of our heart filled with Christ, there's simply no room for expectations to promote themselves as more important than God's perfect plan. Will you join with me? Let's start by giving up on measuring up. Then we'll let go of our expectations, embrace imperfection, and accept God's grace for the perilous journey of motherhood.

Let's become unsupermommies together.

An Unsupermommy's Imperfect Plan

1. Give up on measuring up. Accept that God doesn't want you to be the perfect mom.

2. Actively trust God to meet all your needs.

3. Expect to receive God's superpowers in your moments of imperfection.

Releasing Expectations for Baby's Sleep

ive years ago, I was very pregnant with my first big baby boy. As I eagerly awaited his birth, women felt compelled to rub my burgeoning belly and regale me with incomprehensible tales of newborn baby sleep ... or lack thereof. They warned me that my baby would wake up every four hours to eat. I couldn't even comprehend the exhaustion of spending thirty to forty-five minutes awake to feed my baby several times each night. In my ignorance I assumed it wouldn't happen to me. I read that newborns slept sixteen to eighteen hours a day. Surely I could manage a total of eight hours if my baby was getting eighteen! I *knew* my baby would sleep through the night in six to eight weeks. I could handle anything for six weeks, right?

I had no idea.

Then Isaac came. He was not the soft, cuddly, cooing lamb I expected. He was a lion, ravenously hungry and constantly roaring. When he awoke, he was up. He would sleep an hour, then be up for at least two, sometimes three, before going back to sleep. I spent endless hours rocking him, singing old hymns with a quivering voice as tears streamed down my face. Between fluctuating hormones and sleepless nights, I hit rock bottom.

The relentless tears only perpetuated my exhaustion. In my desperation, I searched for hope in the wisdom of the world. I figured there must be a sleep method that could help me overcome this first obstacle of motherhood, but I couldn't get him sleeping long enough to put one into practice. I told my husband I was drowning. Poor man, there was almost nothing he could do. He tried to lull Isaac back to sleep, but because he couldn't provide Isaac with any food, it rarely worked. It had to be me. I did what a mother was supposed to do: I got up and rocked my son over and over while my heart rebelled with anger and unbelief.

Around ten months of age, Isaac began to sleep through the night occasionally. Sleep got better from there, until I had my two babies within thirteen months of each other. I have not had consistent, good sleep for over two years. That's what happens when you get pregnant five months before your baby is ready to sleep through the night. Some say the feeling is hard to describe, but I found a word for it: *exhausted*. I told my husband, mom, friends, and especially myself several times every day, "I am *exhausted*."

I had a two-year-old and a six-month-old and was struggling through the first (*exhausting*) trimester of my third pregnancy. I had every reason to wallow in my *exhaustion*, right? Wrong. It took an immense act of trust to give up the word *exhausted*, but I released it to God. He would see my need; he would fill it.[1]

Guess what happened. No, I didn't stop being tired, but I stopped feeling the emotional turmoil present in the word *exhausted*. Instead I relied on God's mercies, new every early morning. Great is his faithfulness.

Sleep Is a Big Deal, but God's Power Is Bigger

I know, mommies, we need sleep. God wired us this way. Sleep consistently reminds us that we aren't God. God doesn't need sleep but we do. He will not let your foot be moved; he who keeps you will not slumber. Behold, he who keeps Israel will neither slumber nor sleep (Psalm 121:3–4).

Sleep is not important because we need it, but because God doesn't need it. One of the purposes of sleep is to humble us and remind us that we aren't God. If we fixate on how little we are getting, we miss the point completely. Our sleep, or lack thereof, should constantly remind us of our need for God's power to sustains us. We must obsess less over our rest and expect God to provide.

Weren't we talking about expectations for your baby getting enough sleep? Your baby's sleep and your sleep get so tied up together. Your baby's sleep means rest for you, and that emotional need for your own sleep gets tied up in your desire for your baby to sleep. Of course, there are times when sleep obsession really is about the baby. The baby is miserable and run-down and just needs rest.

But if we really level with ourselves, most of the time we hope for the baby to sleep for our own comfort. A desire for sleep is a God-given part of our humanity, so of course a desire for your baby and yourself to rest is a healthy feeling, but it warps quickly when the desire becomes classified as a need. Remember, sleep can never meet your need for rest; only God holds that power.

When God takes the comfort of rest from our bodies, we frenzy against his sovereignty. Our desire for control combined with our tendency to think we know best usurps our belief in his bountiful goodness and sows anger and unbelief in our hearts. Anger is a horizontal sin. It doesn't stay put inside you, instead popping out in every relationship you have.

Before motherhood, I rarely dealt with anger. Then a little baby came to live with me and steal all my personal comforts. At least, that's what my anger told me. If Isaac would only sleep, everything else in my life would be easy. Because I blamed someone else for my problems, anger was a natural result. I wanted to be a good mom, and that's a lot of work. If I was going to meet all of my expectations for motherhood, I needed a lot of sleep.

If I didn't sleep, I would never have enough energy to achieve supermommy status. I told myself that all it would take was a little more sleep to be a good mom, wife, friend, and Christian. If I had more sleep, I could read my Bible, exercise, make dinner, call a friend, clean the house, or take the baby to the zoo. My baby was keeping me from even being a functional mom, and it made me so angry. I transferred all the responsibility for my actions to my sleepless baby. I assumed my circumstances were the problem, rather than my failure to look to God as my source of rest.

Unbelief works in the heart to create a barrier in your intimacy with God. When you refuse to believe you can do life with only a few hours of sleep, you're forgetting God's promises. God told us that **his divine power has granted to us all things that pertain to life and godliness** (2 Peter 1:3).

Dear Mommy, God sees you and he knows what you need. You may think that with different circumstances, you could be supermommy, but God promises that he has already equipped you for godliness right in your current situation. All you need to do is rely on his super-powered grace instead of your own strength. Your sleep and your baby's need for rest fall under his sovereignty. Your struggle isn't being overlooked by God. Even if you're running on just a few hours every night, God knows exactly what you need. He's still equipping you, just not with your own power but with his. On our own power, we may manage to complete the tasks of motherhood with very little sleep, but we certainly won't do them in a life-giving and godly way. The only way to have life and godliness is to find your rest and power in God alone.

God tells you to **trust in the LORD with all your heart, and do not lean on your own understanding. In all your ways acknowledge him, and he will make straight your paths** (Proverbs 3:5–6). Human understanding says if you get enough sleep, you can be a good mom. Trust says that God knows your needs and your baby's needs, and he will shepherd you through your sleepless fog. God's plan probably isn't leading you to the Mommy Hall of Fame, but you don't really need that. His path always leads you precisely to the one thing you can't live without: more of him.

Give up your exhaustion to El Shaddai, the God who sustains you. He knows your needs. He sees your physical and mental exhaustion. Will you believe?

God's Practical Grace for Better Rest

Find rest in God, not in sleep. **Come to me, all who labor and are heavy laden, and I will give you rest** (Matthew 11:28). Sleep is good, but peace is better. Pray each night for God to multiply your few hours of sleep into extra rest for your body. My overactive brain is difficult to calm down for sleep, so I pray Isaiah 26:3 as I get ready for bed: **You keep him in perfect peace whose mind is stayed on you, because he trusts in you.**

Perfect peace comes from a mind that rests in the promises of God. Trust God with today's cares and tomorrow's worries. Let your mind be steady in his promises, and peace will come. A peaceful heart is far more restful than sleep.

Since sleep isn't your sustainer, stop counting the hours. *It's 5:30 a.m. I have been with my baby for an hour, and I am starting to worry about tonight's sleep total. How many hours have I slept so far? When will my toddlers wake up? If I am back in bed in the next half hour, could I get at least one more hour of sleep before another one wakes up?*

Oh, my dear frantic heart, sleep won't lead to wholeness or happiness. In fact, this obsession with counting the hours not only leads to terrible rest, but it also forgets that God's grace is waiting to sustain us every day.

A restful heart is a humble heart. When your heart is humbly accepting God's sovereignty over you and your baby's sleep, you can try new sleep methods without putting your hope in them. Be vigilant in praying for wisdom and patience to help your baby find a routine that works for both of you. A humble heart is willing to adjust priorities. Stop watching pointless TV or reading that engrossing book an hour before you think you should be in bed. Ask your husband to take your phone away at a certain time each night. Choose a nap over a homemade dinner. Takeout, sandwiches, or "brinner" will do just fine. When necessary, a humble heart asks for help. Call on grandmas, BFFs, sisters, cousins, babysitters, and husbands. Some days you need a break from your baby for the sake of rest. You can't do it on your own. Eat a little humble pie and let someone bless you with the gift of a baby-free afternoon.

Dear Exhausted Mommy, when you unplug from the expectation of good sleep, you'll receive freedom from anger and unbelief. You'll be able to connect to God's power to energize you when the hours of sleep are few and far between. Then humble your heart to receive help from others so you can find more rest. Plug in to God's truth and you'll be filled with God's sustaining superpower despite an imperfect night's sleep.

An Unsupermommy's Imperfect Plan

1. Defeat the sins of anger and unbelief by trusting that God knows your needs and will not fail to meet them.

2. Make practical plans to get more sleep, then entrust them to God's sovereignty.

3. Remember that sleep is good but God's peace is better.

Releasing Expectations for Feeding Your Baby

My friend just dropped by to pick up some brewer's yeast. No, she's not a home brewer, just a mom struggling through that newborn grind. Actually, brewer's yeast is an essential ingredient in lactation cookies. It's a genius idea: a recipe for bumping up your milk production—and wait, it's a cookie! I love them. I'm not breastfeeding, but I'm still tempted to whip up a batch.

My friend had her kiddos in the car, but it only took me a moment to register that she needed to talk. Her second baby was about twelve weeks old, and she was breaking down—struggling with breastfeeding, yes, but also with her life. Because when you're struggling with breastfeeding, it *becomes* your life.

As we chatted, her story spilled forth with her tears: her baby was fussy and difficult, breastfeeding was a battle, and she couldn't manage to get dinner on the table or clean her house. I looked into her pain-filled eyes and my heart broke.

I knew the desperation behind them all too well. She wasn't trying to be a supermommy; she was struggling to meet the immediate needs of her baby and three-year-old.

When you have a baby, life becomes survival mode. You can't manage to cook a meal or wipe down your kitchen counters. When your baby is full of needs, life must pause to meet them. When your baby's most basic need—to eat—is a battle, all other life halts. Every woman fighting this battle must choose the path that's right for both mom and baby.

For some women, the right road is putting everything else on hold and making breastfeeding their only daily task. For other women, it's the emotionally charged choice to use formula. Some women even master an artful combination of pumping, breastfeeding, and formula. I want to let you in on a little secret: all these choices can be right. None of these choices makes you a bad mom or a supermommy.

There is a Christian tendency to equate breastfeeding with godliness. Breastfeeding is selfless, sanctifying, demanding work. I can't say enough good things about women who choose to give of themselves so fully to feeding their child. It's not just the physical work (of which there is plenty); it's also the emotional and psychological task of sacrificing your body for another six months, twelve months, eighteen months, or more.

So bravo to breastfeeders! God created an amazing thing when he invented breast milk. The intricacies of how breast milk adapts and changes to the needs of the child should make us praise God. He deserves all the glory for this part of creation that is so complex that science is unable to replicate it or even understand it.

On the flip side, let's be vigilant not to exchange worshiping the Creator with worshiping the creation. The Bible affirms nursing and giving nourishment to your child, not specifically the act of breastfeeding. A mother must seek God's wisdom for how to best do that for her child. For the mother struggling with this choice, know that breastfeeding is just one of many good things you can prioritize in your relationship with your baby. If you choose it as a priority, it will consume much of your time. If you choose a different priority, other good things will take its place. Either way, no one will have time to be a supermommy.

There are three common breastfeeding scenarios. The first is the most unusual: a woman has a baby, goes through minor struggles, and breastfeeds happily for a year or more. The second scenario is that a woman has a baby and has to work diligently to provide to her child the blessing that is breast milk. Eventually the struggle lessens for many women, but for some it is a hard job every … single … day.

The third scenario is the most emotionally charged. I know; it happened to me three times. A woman gives birth. She wants to breastfeed. She prays to breastfeed. She earnestly seeks wisdom and tips to create a healthy breastfeeding relationship between her and her child, but she faces many problems and eventually decides it is best to bottle-feed, using her own milk or formula.

The first two scenarios are a desire fulfilled, which often leads to the pitfall of pride. The woman in the third scenario deals with pride's sneaky twin, shame.

Nursing Mamas, Keep a Careful Eye on Your Heart

Our culture is bursting with information on the benefits of breastfeeding, support from professional lactation specialists, and peer support groups. Yes, there is still debate about public breastfeeding, and pumping in the workplace is a difficult journey, but a woman in America can't go through pregnancy or early motherhood without frequently hearing the benefits of breastfeeding for both mother and child.

I'm glad there is support for breastfeeding moms, but the "breast is best" culture must be navigated with God-given humility. If a mom forgets God's sovereignty over breastfeeding, she will elevate breastfeeding from undeserved blessing to a result of her own hard work.

It's true that breastfeeding moms must sacrifice daily for their child to receive food. This perpetual act of servanthood is the Christian way, isn't it? But a mother's heart can soon begin to swell with pride in her hard-earned accomplishment. It isn't too far of a stretch to believe in our hearts, if not our heads, that breastfeeding is the mark of a good Christian woman. Unfortunately, this mistaken pride makes breastfeeding into a path for earning the approval of other Christians and even the approval of God.

Breastfeeding is a beautiful gift, but how easily our sinful hearts twist it into something dangerous. A breastfeeding friend once acknowledged to me that when she saw another mom bottle-feeding, she felt simultaneously proud and jealous. She was jealous of the mother's ease of feeding her baby in a public place and ability to allow another person to feed her baby, but she also felt proud that she soldiered through the difficult days and sleepless nights to provide her baby with the benefit of her breast milk.

My friend had a good desire to breastfeed, and she persevered through countless hours of struggle to receive the fruit of a healthy baby. Of course, her human heart defaulted to pride. It was all too easy to forget the true source of her strength. God created breastfeeding. He is the source of all nourishment for babies. He graciously walks with moms through the tears and trials necessary to feed their babies. Only in his sovereign plan does a mom achieve breastfeeding success. Therefore, let the one who boasts, boast in the Lord (2 Corinthians 10:17).

Dear Milky Mommy, make your success, your struggle, or your failure at breastfeeding an occasion to proclaim God's goodness to the world.

Bottle-Feeding Moms, Don't Live in Shame

If you're a mom wallowing in her breastfeeding failure, it's time to let yourself off the hook. I failed at breastfeeding … three times. Even after three babies and a lot of processing with God, a seed of sadness lingers. Successful breastfeeding simply remains a desire unfulfilled. It wasn't the path I planned, but in God's grace I'm content with it. You can be too. God asked you to walk this road. He didn't make a mistake. Don't let your mind run crazy in the land of what-if. What if I had tried this supplement? What if I had attended La Leche League? What if I'd had an unmedicated birth?

Let me break the bondage of your what-ifs: none of it would have made a difference. God is sovereign over how your baby eats, which means God has control over your breast-feeding experience, not you. I don't mean that we shouldn't use the copious amounts of wisdom to create the most likely path of success in breastfeeding. I mean that there is no magic formula for breastfeeding—or any aspect of mothering—that guarantees success every time. God will use this failure for good, for you and your baby. That's how God's sovereign will works. He uses circumstances in our lives to direct our paths to him, and closer to God is always for our good.

Feeling ashamed of not breastfeeding is a result of elevating a good desire to the throne of your heart. God used bottle-feeding to demonstrate my inability to do motherhood in my own strength. Without the outside help of bottles and formula, I literally wouldn't have had the capacity to provide food for my children. Talk about humbling! My inability to breastfeed was like a neon arrow pointing me to the truth that, ultimately, God is the one who provides for and sustains the life of my baby.

I wasn't enough to sustain my babies, but God provided me a means to nourish them. In the same way, God gave Paul a thorn in the flesh to make Paul aware of his own weakness. Then God told him the most amazing news: My grace is sufficient for you, for my power is made perfect in weakness (2 Corinthians 12:9). Let that truth sink in. We bring weakness to God, and he demonstrates his power perfectly through it! Sign me up for that!

God's power and grace in our lives always trumps the opinions of others. We may have failed at breastfeeding, but God won't fail to nurture our child's growth. May the trying experience of not breastfeeding send you not to shame, but to your knees. Humility in motherhood is always a gift from God. Take the experience of being humbled in your own ability to provide food for your baby and apply it to every part of your mothering experience. We can't always protect and nurture our children, but God can. When we fail our children, God's there. He's their ultimate source of protection and nurture. Let's not boast in our power as mothers, but in God's power to sustain all of creation.

• If you fall into the pit of shame, remember two things. First, God accepts you in all your weakness. He wants to use your weakness as an occasion to demonstrate his power. Second, shame is the result of perceived judgment, but others grant us far more grace than we imagine. The woman nursing her baby at the park while you bottle-feed may be staring because she yearns for the freedom of bottle-feeding. The grandmother at the grocery store may look twice at your bottle because she remembers her own struggle with breastfeeding. Yes, there will be some who judge you for bottle-feeding your child, but there will probably be fewer than you think.

Fellow bottle-feeder, don't live in shame for failing the world's standard of motherhood. For am I now seeking the approval of man, or of God? Or am I trying to please man? If I were still trying to please man, I would not be a servant of Christ (Galatians 1:10).

Shame is the result of elevating the opinion of others above the approval of God. Other people may be vicious and judgmental, but God is kind and loving. Put the venomous judgments aside and focus on God's gentle love calling you to freedom and redemption by the blood of Jesus. Embrace the Bible's standards for your life. The glory of the gospel is that when you fall short of God's perfect law, Jesus stands in the gap of your imperfection. Jesus writes his perfect name in blood over every failure, redeeming all your wrongs. No more shame, only freedom.

Dear Broken Mommy, if you choose to bottle-feed, spend less time worrying about what matters to other people and more time focused on what matters to God. Breastfeeding is a good desire, but it's not a God desire. If you are unsuccessful, replace it with more time spent creating a home that shepherds your children to God. Less of us, more of God—that's the ultimate goal of the unsupermommy.

Mommy-To-Mommy, Can We Make a Deal?

If we see another mom feeding her baby, toddler, or even teenager differently from us, let's give her the benefit of the doubt. Let's stop placing the burden of our convictions or experience onto the shoulders of others. We don't know each other's stories until we ask. When we see another woman's pain, let's help bear her burden instead of adding to it. Together we can change stigmas attached to mothers who feed their babies differently. We can start a revolution simply by assuming the best of our fellow mommies.

An Unsupermommy's Imperfect Plan

1. Make a plan for feeding your baby, but receive God's grace if your path changes.

2. Trust in God's ability to provide the proper nourishment for your baby.

3. Resist pride if you breastfeed and shame if you don't.

4. Give each other grace. We might not all feed our children the same way, but let's trust our fellow moms to feed their children in love.

Releasing Expectations for a Superbaby

No sooner is your baby out of the womb and some well-meaning friend will ask, "Do you have an easy baby?" You may be pregnant and dreaming of the blissful possibility that God will gift you with one of these superbabies. You may have a sleepless, screaming newborn in your arms right now and be hoping that one day your baby will undergo a miraculous transformation. Maybe if you do all the right things, your baby will start to act in all the right ways.

The myth of the superbaby paints an image of a child who rarely cries, then only with a sweet soft coo. This baby sleeps through church, breastfeeds quickly, and loves tummy time. The superbaby always meets milestones just a little early—not too early to be inconvenient but just early enough for grandma to brag about it. As superbabies mature into supertoddlers, they manage to be confident but wary of strangers, playful but ready to share, and always willing to clean their plates.

Let me go ahead and dash your wildest dreams. Just as the supermommy is an impossible standard set by ourselves and our culture, the superbaby is also a myth. Your babies won't always do what you have so carefully planned for them. Your babies will not meet every milestone by the earliest age. Your babies will not eat, sleep, play, learn, and flourish in the same way as your friends' babies. Babies are their own complicated little persons, not a reflection of our perfect parenting practices.

My first baby was tough, as all first babies feel at the time. (In comparison to my second, however, he was like dancing through a spring meadow.) He was always, always hungry, and he pulled that whole days-and-nights-messed-up thing for the first few weeks. He was ten months old before he slept through the night. Poor child, he was always hungry, and that makes a baby cranky.

At six months old, he wore size eighteen-month clothing. I couldn't believe how big he was and how much work it was to keep him fed. He met all his physical milestones late: sat up at seven months, crawled at eleven months, and didn't walk until fifteen months. His speech was slow to develop too. Isaac still tends to hit milestones late, but I know him now. His tender heart is afraid to try new things until he is sure he can master it. He hates failing, especially in front of others.

Baby boy #2 didn't meet any of the standards of a good

baby, and he didn't care. Zander never cried … because he was too busy *screaming*. He started screaming the moment he was born, and he never got the message that he should stop. Even when he was happy, his "squeals of delight" were more of the blood-curdling-scream variety. His wails put the whole family on edge.

A screaming baby is like rubbing sandpaper against your soul. It was tough to keep my cool. Zander was definitely no superbaby. He is still a handful, but I know about his passion now. When he likes something, he loves it. When he doesn't like something, he hates it. And when he does anything, he knows exactly the way he wants it done.

When I was pregnant with baby #3, I petitioned God relentlessly for an easy baby. If anyone ever needed an easy baby, it was me in my crazy three-in-three-years situation. When Judah came out, snuggled on my chest, and immediately fell asleep, I thought I had finally received the mythical superbaby. Compared to the first two, he was like a day at the spa—if a spa woke you up every three hours and smelled like the inside of a Dumpster. But he was still easier than the other two.

Here's the truth of it though: even my easiest baby wasn't truly easy. For one month, he screamed and arched his back every time I put him to sleep. He was well over twenty pounds, but the only way to get him to sleep was to hold him firmly against my body and do bouncing squats all around his room. No baby can be a superbaby all the time. As Judah became a toddler, I learned that he has fewer opinions than his older brothers, but when he does care about something, he believes it passionately and persistently.

I'm convinced that God gave me three kids in such quick succession because I needed to be humbled. Three boys in three years was like a knockout punch to accomplishing anything in my own strength. I've always been a very capable person. Give me clear expectations, and I would always find a way to meet or exceed them.

But God had different plans for my motherhood. He didn't want me to be just another capable mother. He wanted me bowed low before the world, raising my tired hands to direct others to him. Everyone who once thought me wise and inspiring can see me here—devastated and fallen, weary and without simple solutions—pointing to the only real solution: Jesus.

Walking through the Fog of Fear

When you want a superbaby more than you want God's plan, the sins of fear and comparison may entrap your heart. In a world of endless information, fear can run rampant in our mommy hearts. We can Google any small developmental delay, sickness, possible symptom of a disability, or inability to meet a milestone, and find an endless list of what might be wrong with our baby. We'll discover all varieties of scary information if we search for it. Although it's not wrong to research, an unhealthy obsession with staying informed is a symptom of fear.

I might not know you personally, Mommy, but I do know that you desperately want the best for your kiddos. You love them so much it's outlandish. Ready to have your mind blown? God loves your children more than you do.

What?

It feels a bit like a crime to even write that down. No one should be allowed to love our kids more than us, right? Thank God that's not true, because our love is imperfect and fallen. God's love is infinitely powerful, sovereign, good, and complete; it's on another level from what our sinful human hearts can hold. His love is not godly or Christlike. It *is* God. It *is* Christ. It is everything our child needs. If God loves our kids like that, we are compelled to trust him with them. "If you then, who are evil, know how to give good gifts to your children, how much more will the heavenly Father give the Holy Spirit to those who ask him!" (Luke 11:13).

God knows your child better than you do. God knows what your child needs the most: more of him. It's time for our mommy hearts to entrust our children to God's tender care. Don't be afraid of the bumps in your child's life. The very problem that we so desperately want to save our children from may be the experience that drives them to their knees.

When you're tempted to fear, trust God instead. "Fear not, for I am with [your child]; be not dismayed, for I am your [child's] God; I will strengthen [your child], I will help [your child], I will uphold [your child] with my righteous right hand" (Isaiah 41:10, brackets added). Recount God's faithfulness—to yourself and your baby. I don't mean in your head. If you're going to fight fear with God's faithfulness, grab a pen and make a list! You will be surprised by how much God has already been active and present in your baby's life. When you know specifically how God has been faithful in the past, it's so much easier to trust him with your baby's present and future.

Remember that God loves your child even more than you do. God loved that child so much that he sentenced his own Son to an excruciating death. God turned his face away from his own Son covered in your child's sin so he could turn his face toward your child. Such an amazing love!

Living without the Comparison Parasite

It's wonderful to have a group of fellow mommies around you, but that also opens that big old nasty can of worms called comparison. My boys were born in a swarm of babies. From the time I got pregnant with my first son to the time I had my last, thirteen babies were born to either a sibling or a best friend. If I include all my friends and acquaintances, that number reaches beyond one hundred. I have a lot of babies to compare with mine. I bet you do too, even if it's just the babies in the nursery or the ones clogging up your Facebook feed. It's no secret that this age of social media feeds the comparison parasite.

Many Christian women are wising up to the way comparison eats at our happiness, but few are addressing the root of the issue. *Comparison* is a pretty word that justifies some nasty sins that the Bible calls coveting, jealousy, and envy. Hey, mommies, it matters what we call things. If we're guilty of occasionally comparing ourselves to others, it doesn't sound that harmful. The chance comparison can't be that hard to control by our own power. We can tell ourselves that comparison is just a secret behavior that doesn't harm other people.

But coveting, envy, and jealousy are sins, plain and simple. As a Christian, labeling a sin is actually good news. The Bible is clear that we can't get rid of sin by our own power, but Jesus came to obliterate sin's power over us. There is freedom from an unhappy life of comparison, and it's found not in our power but in Jesus' free salvation.

In the tenth commandment, God admonishes us not to covet anything that belongs to our neighbor—including their baby! The lie behind the sins of discontentment is that we would be better off if we had the things our friends have. I was convinced that if I had my friend's "easy baby" instead of my own, my life would be better. It would be easier to be a good mom, wife, friend, and Christian with a baby like hers. *I would never get angry at that kind of baby. If my baby was easy like that, I would have the energy to be intimate with my husband. I could make my own kombucha and bake my own bread, if only I had a baby like hers.* The more my life as a mom deviated from my plan, the deeper I buried myself in the lies of discontent.

Pride assumes that our circumstances spark our sin. Our prideful hearts are wrong. It's not our circumstances, but the unsurrendered desires within us. Instead of hoping for a change of circumstances, remember that God gives you everything you need for life and godliness—with *your* house, *your* job, *your* kids, and *your* husband. Ultimately, you don't need a change of circumstances; you need a change of heart.

The other lie behind the sins of discontentment is that another woman's life is only the summation of all the grace you see in it. Through the lens of social media or the chit-chat of play dates, we often only see the blessed portions of another woman's life. If you could see her life as a whole, it's unlikely you would want to trade your problems for hers. Maybe you're jealous of your friend whose baby is an amazing napper. Would you still feel that way if you knew she was battling postpartum depression? Maybe God gave that good sleeper to her as grace to weather the storm of her depression. The point is that we never know the entire story or why God imparts specific graces to others and not to us. All

I know is that God gives *me* specific grace for *my* circumstances, not for another's.

When you envy and covet the graces of another, you're ignoring the full picture—that each grace given by God is a tool in his redemptive plan for the person he grants it to, not for you. Remember, God gives to each of us abundantly, when none of us deserves it. The happy truth is that the friend with the "easy baby" doesn't deserve what she has been given and neither do you. We're all on the same plane—sinners saved by grace—and every gift, every joy, every triumph we receive is just grace. Blessings are not a result of what we do; instead they play specific roles in our sanctification story.

Gifts of grace work together with our trials and hardship to create one complete picture of God's redemption of our lives. I don't want another mom's trials, so I shouldn't covet her graces either. They wouldn't do me any good. I have my own suffering and trials, and I need my own specific grace to cover them.

The only antidote to coveting everything under the sun—or online—is contentment. Contentment is not focusing on what you have—be it the perfect family, a happy season of life, or a good job or house or circumstances—and saying it's enough for you. Contentment is experiencing joy because God is with you in your current circumstances, good or bad. **Keep your life free from love of money, and** be content with what you have, for he has said, "I will never leave you nor forsake you." So we can confidently say, "The Lord is my helper; I will not fear; what can man do to me?" (Hebrews 13:5–6).

The secret to contentment lies in understanding God's ever-present support in every circumstance. Because he never leaves us, we can have his joy despite our current trials. According to Elisabeth Elliot, "The secret is Christ in me, not me in a different set of circumstances."[1] More of Jesus is the secret key to a content heart.

Contentment isn't something that can be mastered, then ignored. Paul knew that contentment would be a constant battle where we would easily feel defeated. So he wrote, I can do all things through him who strengthens me (Philippians 4:13). Paul's context for this verse isn't battling sin or finding strength in God when faced with trials. The context of this powerful verse is the battle for contentment. I'm not saying it can't be applied to other battles, but Paul specifically recognized the importance of this biblical truth in application to contentment. In our own strength, a content heart is impossible, but with God's superpowers, all things (even contentment over comparison) are possible.

Make contentment a daily focus because it's a daily battle. Meditate on contentment-producing Bible verses. Put them on your walls, your mirrors, and your dashboard. Preach to yourself the truth of God's abundant and specific grace. Redeem your discontented grumblings into shouts of praise.

One final thought about coveting and comparison: As women, we need to be especially careful about inviting comparison from our friends. You are not ultimately responsible when a friend covets your set of circumstances, but you can take steps to support others as they fight against this sin. I love sharing about my children. I clearly love sharing about my experience of motherhood or I wouldn't be writing this book.

Sharing can be loving and insightful or it can be icky and sinful. Some loving sharing may lead our sisters in Christ to covet, but more often it's the sharing that comes from a boastful heart that invites comparison. Sharing our motherhood experiences easily morphs into boasting if our heart attitude is pride in our child's accomplishments instead of gratefulness for the gift God has given in that child. It's a tricky line, boasting in God as the giver of good gifts instead of boasting in your child. A couple of key questions can help us discover our heart motivations:

1. Am I believing or implying that I did something deserving of this special child?
2. Does the way I am sharing this give the glory to God as the Creator or to me as the parent?
3. Would I feel encouraged or discouraged if a friend shared this with me?

If we all practiced asking these questions before we posted to social media or gushed via text, phone, or even in person to a dear friend, we wouldn't necessarily share less, but we would share better. Can you make your sharing a place where an unsupermommy is pointing to her super-powered God? God wants to use you to be a light for his glory instead of your own. Will you let him?

Practical Grace for Unsuperbabies

Giving grace begins with you. Your baby not living up to a superbaby standard isn't a fault of your motherhood. You're not the reason your child fails to meet a milestone. You're not the reason your baby doesn't want to try solids or your toddler has separation anxiety. Give yourself grace by refusing to compare your motherhood with that of mothers around you. You're not perfect, but your imperfections are part of God's path for you and your child.

Letting go of expectations for yourself will create an atmosphere of grace within your home. Next, extend copious amounts of grace to your children. When one of her grandbabies cries, my mom often comforts them with a loving embrace and a pouty voice as she says, "It's not easy being a baby."

The old adage is true. It's not easy to be a baby. They're trying so hard to adapt to this wild new world around them, and we have so many expectations for their behavior. Don't let your relationship with your baby begin with your disappointment. Create a place where imperfection is met with unconditional love. Your response to your baby's failures is their first glimpse of the grace God lavishes on us.

Dear Proud Mommy, we aren't perfect, and neither are our children. Their very imperfections make them unique little people who we have the privilege to shepherd through our own inadequacies. If they were superbabies, they wouldn't need their super-powered God.

An Unsupermommy's Imperfect Plan

1. Allow God to work his power in your baby's imperfections. He loves your baby. Recount examples of his great faithfulness when fear threatens your peace.

2. Identify comparison as the sins of discontentment: envy, coveting, and jealousy. Make a habit of confessing these sins and accepting God's grace and Jesus' freedom instead of trying to fight comparison with willpower.

3. Never give up in the battle for contentment. Paul says that a content heart is impossible in our own power but can be a reality when Jesus' power works in us.

4. Create an atmosphere of accepted imperfection in your own home by extending grace to your child's imperfections.

Embracing Imperfection: Step 2—Get Connected!

I know this may be a little late in the game, but I have to admit something: I'm not perfect at being imperfect. Some days I still try really hard to be a supermommy. I often let my expectations morph into needs instead of keeping them submitted to God's authority. Even after writing this book, I tend to let my desire to be a "good mom"—by my standards or the world's—become more important to me than my desire for God.

A Conduit for God's Superpower

I have days of failure and days of exhaustion, but they happen less now than they once did. God is growing me and changing me through the process of motherhood. I'm not writing to you because I have it all figured out, but because I don't. I'm not even perfect at accepting my own imperfection, which might be the real mark of an unsupermommy. I can't even embrace imperfection by my own strength. Sin is simply too twisty. It's hard to nail down, and it's impossible to defeat by myself. *Oh, God, I need you. Every hour, I need you!* The gospel is my lifeline every day, every moment. Without it, I am powerless, trapped in my own obsession with meeting expectations.

Imperfection may feel like failure, but it's actually an opportunity for freedom. If we were perfect, the cross of Christ would be emptied of its power (see 1 Corinthians 1:17). Our failures, laid at the feet of the cross, are the starting place for God's power in our lives.

Fellow Mommy, we can't change our circumstances, but we can change how we experience them. There are too many expectations for us to ever achieve perfection as a mom. We will never be supermoms, and we can't change that.

But we *can* boast in our weaknesses as an opportunity for the power of Christ to rest on us. That's the great paradox of the Christian life. God takes the foolish, the broken, the weak, and the sinful, and uses them for his glory and his power to shine through. But we have this treasure in jars of clay, to show that the surpassing power belongs to God and not to us (2 Corinthians 4:7). Jesus is the treasure; we're simple jars of clay, the perfect backdrop for God to demonstrate his glory.

Ultimately, the point of motherhood isn't to raise our babies; it's to find Jesus and show him off to everyone around us. Hear me, Mommy, your baby isn't your life. Your experience as a stay-at-home mom, working mom, or single mom isn't life. Your house and your husband are not life. Jesus is life. If you know Jesus, you have the golden ticket.

God wants us to both connect to his power source and act as conduits to let his power flow to others. We don't have the power to be supermommies, but let's be conduits for God's superpower. All we have to do is connect to God's power, charge up with his grace, and ignite our world with overflowing joy. Living in God's power doesn't lead to perfection, but it does lead to victory!

Creating Our Connection

It was one of those days when I felt stuck in the backseat of my own life. The baby sat in the driver's seat, and I was along for a really crazy ride. He had been up all night, so I had been up all night, and still he wouldn't sleep. He was too exhausted to rest, and everything I tried was the wrong thing. He didn't want his bottle, and he didn't want food. He didn't want to be rocked, and he didn't want to play. His crying mess of a life was contagious.

I just couldn't keep it together. I vacillated between tears and anger. I told him in no uncertain terms that he would do what I needed him to do *or else*. (If you've ever tried to threaten a baby, save you your breath. It doesn't work.) I begged him to eat and sleep, with tears streaming down my face. All my threatening and pleading just led to more tears for both of us. We were one giant slobbery mess.

I tend to blame that kind of day on my babies. Obviously, if my world was right, then I would be happy and confident. I've learned something through writing this book: if my emotions run high and wild and I feel out of control, I'm plugged in to the wrong thing. If not achieving one of my good desires leaves me devastated, I'm plugged in to the wrong thing. I'm looking to my baby, my husband, my friends, my home, or some other imperfect energy source for peace and life. These good things may be blessings, but they aren't a power source. They don't provide life—only God does.

The people around us can't provide us with the power we need, and we can't find it inside ourselves. We were never made to be battery operated, pulling from our own power. We must unplug from our own insufficient determination and expectations, and connect to the only true source of superpower. When we find ourselves at the end of our ropes moment after moment and day after day, we have to stop trying to run on batteries. In our weakest moments, connecting to God gives us endless power. All we have to do is accept his strength over our weakness—simply get connected.

The busier we get, the more essential it is to not get unplugged. It's like when your phone is running every app in the background while playing a podcast and downloading some videos for the kids. It's doing a lot, so it needs to stay connected to power throughout the day. It can't just get thirty minutes in the morning and ten minutes before bed. That busy phone is going to need to be plugged in all day.

You're running a whole bunch of apps at the same time: housekeeper, nurse, teacher, accountant, cook, friend, caretaker, entertainer, and more, and they're constantly running. You must stay permanently connected to God's superpower.

The Bible has a special term for staying connected: *abide*. In John 15, Jesus calls himself the vine. If we don't stay connected to the vine, we're just dead, fruitless branches. I know the term *abide* feels ambiguous, so let me break it down for you.

Take your most important human relationship, whether it be your husband, your mom, or a friend. Now think about how you stay connected to that person throughout your day. Do you spend thirty minutes with that person in the morning and then forget them until bedtime? No, you probably reach out and communicate regularly. You probably think of them often. I bet you talk, text, and e-mail. You probably think about that person too, remembering things you've done together and making plans for the future. I bet that person even impacts your decision making. You consider that person's thoughts and feelings as you go through the routine of your day. All those things are signs of abiding, sticking close to your special person.

Here's the problem: Your very special person isn't a superhero or a power source. Your special person can build you up, but they can't charge you up. You can, however, have that kind of intimate access to superpower by building a relationship like that with Jesus—the only true source of life and power. How do we maintain our connection to God? Chunks of time in communication are great, but small connection points throughout the day are essential.

Just like with your most important person, your relationship to Jesus should inform your day. Decisions, from simple to complex, are made in light of your relationship to God. Your thoughts are constantly being pulled back to him. You connect to him when you need help or wisdom, and his character impacts how you live. You can't pull a branch in and out of its vine and expect it to live a fruitful existence. It has to stay put. All its sustenance must be derived from the unending source of the vine.

Remaining connected can't always mean having our Bible open with a cup of coffee, but don't worry. Staying plugged in doesn't require continuous quiet time. Abiding takes place in our hearts as the physical world continues around us.

For me, continuous connection happens in a few ways: food, water, and air. First comes food, putting in the Bread of Life, which is the truth of the gospel presented through the Bible. This looks like Bible study in the morning, memorized verses repeated over the lies of my mind, and even reading gospel-centered devotionals, Instagram accounts, and blogs. Water is the Holy Spirit, experienced through prayer, worship, and the Word. Air is my experiences. I breathe them into me and let the truth of the gospel transform them through the Holy Spirit's guidance, then I breathe back out into the world a transformed understanding through what God has done in my heart. In these ways, I stay connected to God throughout the chaos of my day. He becomes my very important person.

The Bible explains it this way: Seek the LORD and his strength; seek his presence continually! (1 Chronicles 16:11). Motherhood can feel really lonely, but I assure you that if you seek God continually, you'll find that he is standing right beside you.

If you're stuck in tired-mommy stage, this pattern of abiding may sound exhausting. You may feel too tired to eat, drink, and breathe God. But God's Word assures us, So we do not lose heart. Though our outer self is wasting away, our inner self is being renewed day by day (2 Corinthians 4:16). If you're physically exhausted, it's time to take heart in God's power to renew. Your body and mind may feel like they are falling apart, but all you need to do to receive renewal is stay connected to God. In actuality, you're too tired *not* to search for spiritual food, water, and air, because receiving God's sustenance is the only way you will get un-tired again. You will never have energy for your life if you don't plug in to the only true source of power.

Connecting to God's superpowers is the only ticket to the wisdom you need to navigate the confusing and overwhelming decisions of motherhood. **Do not be conformed to this world, but be transformed by the renewal of your mind, that by testing you may discern what is the will of God, what is good and acceptable and perfect** (Romans 12:2).

If you don't remain connected to God, you'll find yourself conformed to the world's standard of motherhood. If you want to renew your mommy mind and have wisdom to discern God's path for you, you must plug in to his truth instead of to your plans for perfect motherhood. You may be exhausted. You may be overwhelmed. You may be living in moment-by-moment survival. You may be stuck in motherhood-neutral, but that is the very reason that you must stay connected to God. Your life and the life of your baby are dependent on you accessing the unending power of God.

Dear Depleted Mommy, your life doesn't have to stop for you to receive God. Hold your precious world in open arms before the God who built the little world around you. Let the mundane moments of your day and the blessings you receive and the mountains you must climb be a path to knowing God intimately. No need to search farther than the end of your rope to find God's superpower waiting for you.

An Unsupermommy's Imperfect Plan

1. Connect to God. Nothing else provides the power you need!

2. Stop trying to use the dead battery of your own willpower to provide energy for the tiring task of motherhood.

3. Eat God's Word. Drink in the Holy Spirit. Breathe in your circumstances to orient them around the truth of God's Word. In this way, you will let the word of Christ dwell in you richly (Colossians 3:16).

Releasing Expectations for Your Appearance

I need to be up-front with you. I'm nervous about writing this chapter. I'm one of those "naturally thin" people. I just don't want you to see a picture of me online and write this off. I'll admit that before I had children, I was completely ignorant of what it feels like to struggle with body image.

Then I had kids. I gained over forty-five pounds with my first child. I'm a small person, which makes forty-five pounds *significant*. I ate whatever my pregnant hormones craved because I was blissfully unaware of how difficult it is to lose weight. That bit me in my inflated, pregnant butt.

I also didn't breastfeed very long, so I never experienced its supposed magical fat-melting effects. My friend gave birth a month after me and was back to her pre-baby weight in less than two months. You may know women like that; it's best to pretend they don't exist. It took over six months for my thirty-five pounds to come off, and then the last ten pounds took another six months. Post-baby bodies require a lot of grace from the souls walking around inside of them.

Even when the extra weight was finally gone, my body was never the same. I finally got my woman hips, but I'll admit I'm glad I did (I've had too many door-to-door salespeople ask if I could go get my mother). However, I don't care much for my newly broad shoulders or inability to find jeans that stay up without a belt. I gained less weight with baby #2 because I learned my lesson about eating anything and everything, but I still had the last stubborn ten pounds of baby weight left when I got the shocking news I was pregnant again. My weight gain with the final pregnancy added to what was left over from baby #2 and drove me to the heaviest I've ever been.

For the first time, I felt really insufficient when I looked in the mirror. I never had a chance to get out of wearing mostly maternity clothes with my back-to-back babies. I wasn't able to wear most of my clothes—pretty much all the cute stuff—for over two years. I hated looking in the mirror and not recognizing the face staring back at me. I told myself that my pre-baby face was the beautiful one. Even as I lost weight, I found that I still looked different.

The fact is, I'm not the same person I was pre-baby. I care constantly for three little people. They make me tired, they make me dirty, and they make certain that showers are few and far between and makeup is rarely applied. My eyebrows tend to go unplucked, and my legs are often unshaven. I don't look like energetic, carefree Maggie anymore. I look like mom Maggie. My tired eyes and dirty clothes betray my state of motherhood whenever I don't have three little boys in tow.

When I look back on my wedding photos, I see a beautiful young woman blooming with hope and joy and love. But beneath her beautiful surface, I recognize that she didn't know how to hope in God for his grace to meet the physical exhaustion of sleepless nights. That bride hadn't experienced the joy of watching her babies' first giggles. She couldn't imagine the way her love would grow for her husband as she watched him gently rock a hurt child.

I don't want to be that woman anymore. I'm not the same woman wearing that white lace dress. I'm so much more. I don't need to look like her again. I want to look like the new me, spiritually refined by the fires of motherhood. Our outside may not look as "perfect" as it once did, but God is busy renewing our soul. Don't lose heart if you don't look like the woman in the white dress anymore. Find hope in the truth that God is busy remaking you into an imperfect woman who gives glory to her super-powered God.

In *The Nesting Place*, Myquillin Smith challenges women that their homes don't have to be perfect to be beautiful. Hey, Mommy, your body doesn't have to be perfect to be beautiful either. Unless you walk two steps behind an airbrushed hologram of yourself, your body will always be imperfect by society's standards. Breathe deep and accept your body's imperfections, then let God use it as a part of his perfect plan.

Employing an imperfect vessel to serve the perfect plan of a perfect Savior is part of God's gospel story. **How beautiful upon the mountains are the feet of him who brings good news** (Isaiah 52:7). These imperfect mommy-bodies are built to serve God in extraordinary ways. When we embrace God's grace for our physical imperfections, we point our babies to the good news of a perfect God who came to save imperfect people.

Personal Appearance and Control

I never feel less in control of my life than when I'm snuggling a newborn rascal. Try as we may to make them conform to all our awesome baby plans, newborns are mavericks, determined to break every law of the universe. Don't even say the word *schedule* to a new mommy or she may throw you across the room (proving me wrong about her superhuman abilities). When life feels like a spinning whirlwind around us, we grasp for something to control. As women, it's often our bodies.

When we're pregnant, breastfeeding, or continually baby-wearing a colicky, screaming little one, we imagine the day we will regain control over our bodies. We seek out new diets, new exercises, new clothes, new hairstyles, new *anything*, because it feels like the needs of our babies have stripped our beauty and our identity away. Our culture surrounds us with the propaganda that we're in control of our bodies. If we just buy this new cleanse, mascara, or magical nursing wrap dress, we'll be beautiful again.

It drives us to consume more and more as we attempt to maintain an ever-slipping control over the fragile and aging, used and abused bodies we inhabit. We frantically grasp at any product or plan that will put us back in control over our changing and aging bodies.

Paul David Tripp explains, "A desire for a good thing becomes a bad thing when that desire becomes the ruling thing."[1] It's not wrong to care about our appearance, but when it begins to dictate our decisions, consume our thoughts, and activate raging emotions, it has begun to appropriate God's place in our hearts.

This kind of overgrown desire becomes a gospel usurper. It becomes a counterfeit savior. Good desires are no longer good for us when we believe we can't find joy, peace, hope, and happiness without them. Those are surefire signs that they have usurped the truth of the gospel in our hearts. Controlling your appearance—your perfect makeup and hair, slim body, and stylish clothes—will never fill the ache in your soul for acceptance. Acceptance is only found by giving up control over your body to God, who claims you just as you are. Through the work of Jesus, the ugliness of your sin stands beautifully redeemed. Relinquish control to the Master of the Universe and find real joy and peace as an imperfect woman serving a perfect God.

The antidote to assuming control of your body is to remember your status as both created and redeemed. Do you realize that your body is a work of the Trinity? First, the Father created you: **fearfully and wonderfully made** (Psalm 139:14). Next, Jesus redeemed you: **You are not your own, for you were bought with a price** (1 Corinthians 6:19–20). Finally, the Holy Spirit dwells within you: **Or do you not know that your body is a temple of the Holy Spirit within you, whom you have from God?** (1 Corinthians 6:19). God created it, Jesus redeemed it, and the Holy Spirit lives inside of it. Your body matters. Every member of the Trinity plays a role in creating and sustaining it. Don't assume enough ownership to call it ugly or inadequate.

Imagine a famous artist asked you to store one of his valuable works in your home. One day, in the routine of life, the fragile artwork is dropped. There is no way you can fix it, and you feel ashamed of your failure. But the wise artist hears about it and sends his apprentice son to fix the piece. He knows that leaving a piece of valuable art to your failed safekeeping would be a mistake. This time he leaves a guard to protect his art. Do you own that art? Do you control it?

This analogy is imperfect, but I hope it's poking its

silly finger around your brain. If God really is the Creator of the universe, and he really sent his Son to redeem our failure, and he sanctifies us daily through the Holy Spirit living within us, this whole idea of controlling these fragile physical bodies is a myth. We're grasping after a tangible evidence of our own power, when all the power belongs to someone else. Someone who knows us, sees us, created us, and loves us. He bought us with the price of his own body, to free us from control over ours.

Because our bodies are works of the Trinity, God has a triple-vested interest in them. He yearns for us to use these inadequate frames to fulfill his great purposes. May our bodies be tools instead of a stumbling blocks. May they be declared blessed and beautiful, not because of what we do to the outside, but because of how God is sanctifying them from within.

Practical Grace for Our Imperfect Bodies

Let's change our mindset from control to stewardship. Our bodies are essential to serving God in the mission of motherhood.

Stewardship requires grace. If you prioritize dieting and exercise, you need God's grace to not make it about controlling what you look like but about caring for his temple. If you can't manage a strict diet plan, you need grace not to fall into gluttony to fulfill unmet desires or reduce stress. By the same token, caring for our bodies by showering, doing our hair and makeup, and choosing our clothing shouldn't be considered a waste of our valuable time as a mother, but it must remain in check with the needs of our children and other physical needs like food and rest. There is a healthy balance that we can walk as mothers, but we can't walk it alone.

Don't prioritize exercise and healthy eating over time spent in God's Word. Dear One, exercise and healthy eating are beneficial and valuable, but they aren't God. Put diet and exercise in their proper place in your life, and if you can't find a place right now, don't worry too much about it. Body health is a good goal, but it isn't as important as the spiritual health of you or your family.

If going on a specific diet or following a regimented exercise plan is a source of refreshment for you as you struggle through motherhood, then do it. If it's stressful for you and makes life harder, it's okay to skip it for now. Just find times of unstructured movement and start to change daily choices in what you eat to food that nourishes and gives energy rather than creates emotional ups and downs. Don't sway between two extremes. Care for your body in a way that maximizes your energy for the tasks and the time you have on earth to display God's glory to others, but don't do it at the expense of soul renewal through time with God.

We need daily grace to steward our bodies as a resource

God created to bring him glory. It's not a balancing act but a tension. On one side, attempting to control our bodies redirects the glory to us. On the other, apathy over our bodies leaves us tired and unable to complete the physical task of motherhood. We must live in the tension of caring for our physical needs without exalting them into a false gospel. Ultimately, it's a heart issue. Am I eating, exercising, and dressing for the task God gave me or for myself? We think we can control our lives by managing our appearance, but our Creator, Redeemer, and Sanctifier wants to use the physical to accomplish the spiritual.

Dear Imperfectly Beautiful Mommy, the battle over the body begins in the heart. First, we have to give up on measuring up to the world's absurd standards. Next, we have to relinquish control to the One who created, redeemed, and sustains these bodies. Finally, we must not draw strength, beauty, joy, peace, and hope from our physical body, but from God's boundless grace. May Jesus fill our broken jars with the beauty of his glory, for the praise of his holy name.

An Unsupermommy's Imperfect Plan

1. Embrace the motto: Your body doesn't have to be perfect to be beautiful.

2. Accept your new body as evidence of the growth you have experienced as a mom.

3. Remember that God created your body, redeemed your body, and sustains your body. We may not own these bodies, but we're called to be stewards of them.

Releasing Expectations for Your Housekeeping

At the beginning of our marriage, my husband didn't plan for me to stay home after we had kids. His mom worked; therefore, I would work. My mom didn't work after kids, so I sure didn't plan to. Instead of planning my career, I wove the benefits of a wife who stayed home into our everyday conversations. I glossed over the motherhood details since I knew nothing about caring for an infant; instead, I assured him of the glories of coming home to a clean house and a perfectly prepared dinner. I was giving him a load of empty promises, but in my defense, I was naïve enough to think it would be easy to care for our house while our babies napped.

I couldn't have been more wrong.

As I type, my desk is covered with a sheep magnet, a half-eaten granola bar, a Duplo block, and a bill I paid three months ago. Past my desk I see two used spoons, the clothes my toddler wore yesterday, a lone shoe, five puzzles missing pieces, and countless Duplos, trucks, and tractors strewn across the floor. Actually, I'd call this a good day. We (read: my husband) vacuumed last week, and I managed to wipe down half of the kitchen table after lunch. Definitely a good day.

If you're with me right now, this too will pass. If you don't have older kids yet, your mess may look like countless burp rags, unwashed bottles, baby socks, and the lunch you never had a chance to finish. I'm just going to venture a guess that no matter how many children you have or how old they are, your house isn't as clean as you'd like it to be.

I wish I hadn't planned to be the perfect housewife. My unattainable expectations for housekeeping often overshadowed the joy of my first baby's newborn stage. Instead of focusing on meeting his needs and mine, I was obsessed with everything on my list that never seemed to get done. The problem wasn't my needy baby, but that I had the wrong things on my list. If I could rewrite all my lists for that time, they would just say: 1. Baby sleep, 2. Baby eat, 3. Mommy eat, 4. Mommy sleep. Even that list is pretty ambitious. By the time I had my second baby, I had figured out what really needed to be on my list, but by then I was juggling the needs of two little ones. It would never be as simple as it could have been with my first baby.

I'm a lover of lists. Lists are great planning tools, but they can also become roadblocks. I became so committed to my list that it got in the way of life. I focused so closely on the needs of the list that I missed the needs of my family. Finally, when my third baby came, I let go of the list and lived. I took a season off from writing things down. Instead I tried to do one thing every day to make the house a little cleaner than it was. Yes, sometimes I had to intentionally plan to pay the bills or clean the toilets, but I freed myself from the burden of creating a clean house.

As a new mom, I was paralyzed from beginning a cleaning project in case I wouldn't finish before being interrupted by my baby. I drove myself crazy over my inability to make my whole house or even my entire kitchen completely clean. I didn't realize until my third baby that it didn't matter. Now instead of trying to have a completely clean house, I just try to move forward. Cleaning is important, but it isn't urgent.

Rethinking the Proverbs 31 Woman

The Proverbs 31 woman is often upheld as the pinnacle of female Christianity. She definitely sounds like a Christian superwoman: running her own business, cooking meals, shopping with thriftiness, crafting the household décor, gardening, ministering to the poor, teaching other women, and even keeping physically fit.

My dear Aunt Betty is a mother, grandmother, and great-grandmother. She's a thrifty, crafty leader of Christian women. She memorizes whole books of the Bible. She seems like the epitome of the Proverbs 31 gal, but she renounces the use of that woman as the standard for a successful Christian woman. Instead she cautioned me: "You can't do everything the Proverbs 31 woman does in one season of life." I could have kissed her. My dear aunt let me off the hook. No need to be a Christian superwoman when I'm struggling to just be a *decent* mom.

I want to let you off the hook: God gives you specific seasons to accomplish unique tasks. Allow yourself grace for the season of life you're in. Your standards of housekeeping can be different in this season than they will be as your children grow. In fact, your standards for a lot of things must be different for this season. Focus on the most important task before you—raising your kids—and let the other things fall into the small spaces you have left. Your house won't be perfectly clean in that amount of time, but it doesn't need to be.

My Aunt Betty also says, "Some things aren't worth the time it takes to do them well." Do what you can, but don't waste valuable time keeping the perfect house.

But a Pretty House Makes Me Look Pretty Awesome

When I held tight to the unachievable expectation of being a perfect housekeeper, I became buried by an obsession with the approval of others. **For am I now seeking the approval** of man, or of God? Or am I trying to please man? If I were still trying to please man, I would not be a servant of Christ (Galatians 1:10). Pleasing man is a tricky little sin. It lies down deep in the cavern of our hearts, and causes us to do really good things for the absolutely wrong reason.

Have you ever spent an hour cleaning before your friend came over because you didn't want anyone to ever see what your house really looks like? If you're anything like me, an hour spent cleaning your house can barely get the toys off the floor. It's just a drop in the bucket of what really needs to be done.

"I'm sorry my house is such a wreck," you apologize as your friend walks into your tidy foyer. You need that sweet woman to know that this tidied-up mess isn't up to your standards. You want her to understand that you hoped to achieve a magazine-clean home for her enjoyment. Your need for her approval just put not only yourself on the hook for perfection, but your friend as well.

This problem is so pervasive that my best friend and I recently came to the realization that each of us thought the other kept her kitchen really clean. She said, "I guess we have each other sufficiently fooled." We've been best friends for over half of our lives—so why are we still trying to manipulate false impressions of our housekeeping skills?

Let's stop fooling each other and reveal our imperfections to our friends. Since that moment, rather than apologize for how messy my home is, I let a friend know that I did clean for her arrival. I say something like, "I picked up when I knew you were coming. This is so clean for me," or, "I can't believe I had time to clean my kitchen before you came!" May we not let freshly-wiped counters set impossible standards for our friends. Whenever you get a chance, let another woman off the hook of the perfect home.

It's not that you don't clean before a friend comes over, but you do it out of hospitality rather than winning their approval. Don't run away in horror, but there will be times when you absolutely can't get to cleaning the house. As horrifying as it may sound, you should choose to extend hospitality anyway.

I've found that my housekeeping is motivated not just by the approval of my friends but also by the approval of my husband. During my third pregnancy, I was transitioning to the demands of two children while trying to manage the demands of my own pregnant body. Our house reached an all-time low, and my husband graciously offered to hire a cleaning service.

Yes, the same man I had once convinced would receive the benefits of a clean home if only he supported me staying at home with our kids now was offering a cleaning service. The suggestion was a huge blow to my pride. As a stay-at-home mom, I see my job as twofold: caring for our children and managing our household. I want my husband to think that I'm capable and valuable, and I felt like I was neither of those things. This proved that I wasn't capable of balancing the needs of children with the needs of our home. It also wrecked my personal justification that my job at home carried monetary value. We actually needed to pay money out for someone to help me do it.

My sweet husband wasn't judging me; he was serving me. He saw my need and offered a solution to fix it. I was ashamed that he recognized that I couldn't manage my workload, but despite my fears, he didn't think I was lazy or worthless. He saw that I was working as hard as I could and still needed some help.

My shame highlighted my deeply rooted fixation on his approval. My unhealthy focus on his approval instead of God's even impacts our conversations. Like most women, I delight in my husband enjoying a meal I make or remarking on how clean the kitchen looks, but that joy led me to expect that he validates the most mundane housekeeping tasks.

He comes home to a barrage of questions: *Do tacos sound good for dinner?* I ask even though I've already made them. *Did you notice I cleaned the bathroom?* I ask despite the fact he just walked in the door. *Do you know I took all three of the kids to Target with me today?* Of course he knows. He called me in the middle of checkout. These are all small things, and they are all part of my job. Can you imagine how ridiculous this would look in a different profession? It's like a nurse seeking praise from a doctor for inserting an IV correctly. It's a data-entry specialist looking to her coworker for a pat on the back every time she enters a number in her spreadsheet.

Ironically, obsession with the approval of others makes my relationships all about me, me, me. When I need my husband to validate my work, I constantly seek my own needs in our conversations instead of identifying how I can support and value him. It's a futile task. The approval of my husband, children, and friends will never bring satisfaction. True satisfaction only comes from finding God infinitely more valuable than a clean house, a happy husband, or an admiring friend.

I've found that God has taken housekeeping, an area I was so apt to find pride in, and transformed it into my most consistent source for humility. No matter how hard I work at it, my home will always be imperfect when we're living in it. As much as I'd like it to look like a pretty Pinterest image, it's just not how we live. We have a large, open finished basement free of all furniture and full of toys. It seems like no matter how much time I spend on my home, I never quite manage to get the basement picked up.

I've come to think of it as my humble room. The moment my pesky pride starts to beam over our handmade farmhouse table or bask in a friend's praise of my white kitchen, all it takes is a trip down to the basement to be thoroughly humbled. Maybe we all need a space like my basement, where we're constantly reminded that housekeeping perfection isn't attainable or even important.

Keeping an orderly home is a good desire, but it only remains under the authority of God in our hearts when our focus is bringing glory to God instead of ourselves. Paul commends us, **Whatever you do, work heartily, as for the Lord and not for men** (Colossians 3:23). Housekeeping is meant to be about hospitality and stewardship for God's glory instead of earning the approval of others.

When We Reveal Our Imperfections, God Gets the Glory

The only way to lessen the desire for the approval of man is to replace it with a desire for God's glory instead of our own. **"He must increase, but I must decrease"** (John 3:30). We are called to make God's name great in the large world around us, but especially in our small circles of intimacy.

Hospitality and stewardship are the heart motivations that glorify God rather than ourselves through cooking, cleaning, and paying the bills. As mothers, we don't just practice hospitality to the friends and neighbors who enter our home; we also care for our home in a way that creates a healthy, welcoming, comfortable place for our families. The approval of the guests who enter your home, and even the approval of your own family, isn't worth the hours of time spent cleaning, but creating an environment where they feel at peace and accepted can lead their hearts toward God's peace and acceptance. By small efforts you can change a house into a safe haven. That is a goal worthy of your time; the approval of others is not.

Another way to glorify God through housekeeping is through stewardship. God has given us so many good gifts. Are we using them well? As the primary spenders, we must carefully tend to our budget. You can clean as a steward of the home—owned or rented—that God has blessed you with. Identify the good gifts God has given you, and make a point to give them proper care and maintenance.

As you prepare a meal, thank God for his provision for your family and pray for those who will eat it to know him as the ultimate provider. As you launder sheets, rejoice in the comfort they will bring the children who use then. As you pay a bill, consider if it's necessary or if its cost could be reduced in some way. As you clean for guests, remind yourself that the gift of their friendship is worth a little extra effort. In these small ways, you can steward the gifts God has provided for your home without setting your hope on them.

Of course, we can only steward well and have hospitality when we keep our focus on God. This may mean letting dirty dishes crust in the sink while we rest our hearts in the truth of the Scripture. When Mary chose to sit at Jesus' feet rather than serve the guests in their home with Martha, she was commended: "Martha, Martha, you are anxious and troubled about many things, but one thing is necessary. Mary has chosen the good portion, which will not be taken away from her" (Luke 10:41–42).

When life is overwhelming, remember Mary and Martha. Martha may have been the model housekeeper and hostess, but it was Mary whom Jesus applauded. Jesus calls us to spend time in his presence before all else. The one thing necessary isn't a clean house or a healthy meal on the table; it's Jesus. Have you sat with Jesus today?

Dear Hardworking Mommy, there are many things more important than housekeeping, and your life may be filled to the brim with those things these days. Even if you can't find time to wash the dishes today, find time to sit at his feet. I can guarantee you that the feet of Jesus is the only place you'll find complete acceptance and perfect satisfaction.

An Unsupermommy's Imperfect Plan

1. Embrace this season of life as one where a clean house isn't all that important.

2. Let hospitality and stewardship motivate your housekeeping, rather than the approval of others.

3. Allow for imperfect spaces to bring humility instead of shame.

4. Before you spend time on household chores, make sure you have spent time connecting with Jesus, for that is your good portion.

Releasing Expectations for Your Free Time

I bet some of you are rolling your eyes at me right now. Free time? Don't have it. Can't even imagine it. My life is all baby, all the time.

I've been there. I get that feeling. But don't write off this chapter. We all have stolen moments, pinched between the endless needs of our children and the excessive needs of our homes. They can be hard to identify, because a mom's free time doesn't come in the form of binge watching a new TV show or Saturdays at the mall—but trust me, the moments are there. Identify those cracks of time and make them moments of rest. In those small spaces you may reignite your passion for a past hobby or create an intentional plan for regaining a social life.

Those little moments can be places of rest and enrichment or missed opportunities. Take control of them and make them work hard as a space to meet your deepest need: more of Jesus.

I've never been hobby-crazy. My husband has enough hobbies for the both of us. I'm a reader, mostly fiction and magazines. If talking were considered a socially acceptable hobby, it'd probably be my top hit. I didn't feel an overwhelming loss of hobby when I had my first baby, because reading pairs itself particularly well with a newborn lifestyle. Middle-of-the-night feedings gave me a justifiable reason to be up at 3 a.m. with my Kindle in hand. For his first six months, my firstborn didn't nap much except in my arms, so I spent a lot of that time reading. Those stolen moments escaping to another world were one of the few things that kept me swimming forward through that messy, teary, overwhelming season.

Shortly before my first baby, I bought my first smartphone. It was such a gift. I was still working a little for our family business at the time, and that phone allowed me to deal with emails during feedings. An app on it let me make all my Christmas purchases right from the comfort of my nursery rocker. I delved into social media friendships via Twitter. Discovering new apps and new possibilities was entertaining, but it became a black hole for my extra time and energy. I soon discovered the best ways to waste my time on my phone.

Eventually, I rarely read during feedings; I spent the time on my phone. Hours of my life simply wasted doing nothing of value. I have a dear friend who prays as she nurses her children. Now that is time well spent! She will not be called to account for her mental processes during those hours. Eventually my mind grew fat and lazy.

I sat cross-legged on our playroom floor one morning as my kids played on their own (hallelujah!) and I flicked through my daily app roundup. Nothing grabbed my attention and my brain felt numb, paralyzed by the brightness of the screen in front of me. I had become a mental couch potato, so focused on consuming that my mind forgot how to imagine and create.

I needed something to engage my mind during the hours of physical engagement with my children. It was this need along with God's not-so-subtle prodding throughout several areas of my life that began the seeds of this book. If I spent time processing, praying, and chewing over biblical truth as I pushed a train along a track or built the tallest block tower in the world, could I get my mind back in shape? Could I really use my thought life to develop ideas and write something that would help other moms? This book is the fruit of that change in my life.

Mentally-tired Mommy, your phone isn't your hobby. Put it down and discover what you can do with God's gift of brain and body.

Good Hobbies and Bad Hobbies

I'm going to get all black and white here and say there are good hobbies and bad hobbies. A good hobby isn't an escape from your life but an extension of it. A bad hobby is your brain and body in neutral. A good hobby should be worshipful work, because we're made in the image of God. We're by nature creative beings. Even before the fall, Adam was involved in creation through the naming of the animals. God made us to crave meaningful work that makes us an active part in his creation.

As moms, our primary work is raising our kids. Motherhood is such a difficult and meaning-packed job that it's easy to assume that any free time should be spent indulging in the meaningless, as if free time is meant to escape God's calling instead of embrace it.

Hey, Mommies, we don't need an escape from God. We need more of him. Worthwhile hobbies trigger mental, physical, spiritual, or creative stimulation that acts as a guidepost to the source of all rest and replenishment. Amid endless hours of motherhood, our souls feel dry and weak, but Jesus is the Living Water and the Bread of Life. He is the only source of lasting refreshment. If we want our hobbies to give life instead of drain us, we must find what points us to him.

Rest Patterns Must Be Adapted to Life's Seasons

Hobbies come and go with the seasons. As a mother of young children, you may not be able to create handmade cards, but you can color and craft with your kids. You may not be able to read long books, but you can read blogs. You may not be able to run marathons, but you can jog with your kids in the stroller.

My cousin, and best friend, is a new mother of triplets. *Triplets.* Yikes. Her hobbies will certainly be dictated by her current chaos, but they can still be worshipful work. She will need to do shorter, simpler things to find replenishment than a new mother with a baby who sleeps through the night or even a seasoned mother of five.

As your baby grows into a toddler and a child, adapt your hobbies to include them. We lie to ourselves when we believe that enjoyment and rest can only come from time spent away from our children. Motherhood isn't the only thing that defines you, but it is now a core part of who you are. Don't run from your new role; discover how you can develop yourself through it.

Choose Your Hobbies with Intention

As mommies, we can't get all willy-nilly about our free time. We have only moments to spare, so let's use them well! The best way to do this is through goal setting, core values, or a combination of both. I'm not talking about setting specific time-oriented goals. A new mom will never get anything done on a set schedule, but she can still be intentional about how she uses her time. If your goal is to build your relationship with your husband, you'll look for hobbies to do together or ways to bless his needs through your hobbies. If your goal is to be more prayerful, spend your stolen moments cultivating your prayer life.

Goal setting doesn't have to be task oriented; it can simply provide steps for living your life with purpose rather than as a reaction to your circumstances. This isn't as time-consuming as it sounds. The one commodity moms of littles have is plenty of brain space as we complete many mundane tasks throughout the day. Start using your thought life to brainstorm how you can grow in conjunction with mother-hood rather than in spite of it.

Another tool for intentionality is core values. Core values are your essential priorities for how you live. When my husband and I got married, we talked about what we wanted the core values of our marriage to be. A couple of years into having children, we re-evaluated our core values. I expected to adapt them for our expanding family, but we found that the values we originally chose were still exactly what we wanted our family to be about. If you choose core values that are truly at the heart of who you are as a family, they serve as guideposts to direct all major (and minor) decisions.

Because examples are helpful, I will share ours: Glorifying God, Family Togetherness, Learning, Hard Work, and Hospitality. Your core values will probably be completely different because they draw on the essentials of who you are.

The first step is to identify the driving forces behind your vision for your family and then let those things inform your choices for your free time.

Set all your free time on God's throne. What can stay in your new life? What needs to be set aside for this season? What favorite hobbies support your values for you and your family? When will you partake in your hobby?

Many women thrive by giving themselves specific parameters; for example, once the kitchen is clean and I have spent time with God, I can read blogs. Others prefer to create a daily schedule that incorporates periods of both work and rest. Try multiple approaches and discover what works for you in this season.

Relationships Outside of Our Children

I'm a social gal to the core. Two of my top five strengths via StrengthsFinder 2.0 are Woo and Communication. This basically means I love to win people into relationship with me and then gab their ears off. I'm not a baby person, so when I planned to be a stay-at-home mom, I was mostly after the social perks. I imagined a planner bursting with daytime Bible study, mom groups, early childhood classes, and play dates.

The reality was that as a new mom, even the thought of leaving the house drove me to my emotional limit. I couldn't manage feedings and naps well at home, so how would I possibly accomplish them in the midst of social distractions? I eventually forced myself to get out of the house and into a Bible study and the occasional play date, but my friendships survived on only half my brain.

When your baby is with you, your attention will always be divided. That doesn't mean we don't try. It does mean we don't walk into a play date expecting to share all our deepest emotions. It means that we come to Bible study prepared to be summoned out to calm our baby's tears. It means that socializing is still possible, but it won't always be as simple as we hope. We can't set our previous social life as our expectation, but we can discover new ways to have friends we work with this season.

The division of your brain is only one reason that friendships as a mother are hard. If your friends are all having babies too, there is a sense of camaraderie but also a tendency toward comparison. If your friends aren't in the baby-bearing stage, it's difficult for them to understand the division of your attention. Some days you just don't have the emotional energy to be a friend. Other days you crave the emotional companionship of another woman so much that you want to cry.

Past friendships usually change, for better or worse, during the season of young children. Don't worry. Plenty will survive until the other side. New friendships can be difficult to grow and nurture when you constantly have a baby on your hip, but don't overlook the gift of technology. Meaningful, uplifting, Christ-centered friendships can grow over Facebook, Twitter, or text message when in-real-life moments are sparse.

If you're feeling lonely, find some friends to welcome your mess. The best place is women's Bible study. Thank God for the gift of daytime Bible studies with childcare! It doesn't matter if the women at your Bible study are older or younger than you. It doesn't matter if they are unmarried or childless. When you dig into God's Word together, friendship is born.

It can be scary to open up to a new friendship or initiate more spiritual discussion and support into an old one, but meaningful relationships begin with one woman taking a risk. You can be that woman.

On the other hand, if you're feeling overwhelmed by the list of friends you've been intending to do a play date with or the number of Facebook messages you never respond to, I want to let you off the hook. You don't have to feel that way. Friendships must adapt to your new role. Be honest with your friends when you just can't add any more things to your schedule. Don't have a social life at the expense of a happy home life. Don't forget that your inner circle is your most important one.

Last spring, I had to call a season of no play dates for myself. I was discussing it with my best friend and she said,

"I didn't know we were allowed to do that!" Dear Mommy, you're in control of your schedule. You don't need permission from anyone to adjust it or set new parameters. If your child needs a season of no play dates, it's your responsibility as a mother to create it. If you need a season of no play dates, recognize your own needs and don't feel ashamed of them. Just be open and honest with your friends that you or your child needs a break for a while. Most women will admire you. Standing strong for the needs of your family requires boatloads of courage.

There is no question that God ordained your relationships with your husband and your children. They are your first mission field. Other relationships sometimes change with a new season. If the time you spend with others builds you up with renewed energy to walk in the quiet, daily mission of pointing your family to Christ, then it's worth some time away. If instead you constantly give your best self to friends, mentees, or even your Instagram followers, and leave your sinful self to your inner circle, a change must be made.

I'm not saying you should isolate yourself. Never do that! Community is an essential part of our spiritual lives, but there may be seasons when you can only go deep with a chosen few. My current inner circle is by necessity very small. Right now I have room for only my husband, my mom, and my cousin-BFF. I just have a tiny little space for my best friends since childhood, but it's more of a traumatic event encourager than a daily truth-speaking commitment. When your family ministry is overflowing, keep your friend ministry small. There will be time to emerge back into the wider world of discipleship, and God doesn't need your efforts to keep doing his work in the world. First, do the small work God has undeniably placed in front of you.

I find freedom in a few set boundaries. My first boundary is no more than one play date per week. That's all the social life my oldest son can usually handle beyond preschool. Another boundary is that I don't go out without my husband or children more than once a month. I include things like baby showers, neighborhood bunco, or coffee with a girlfriend in this list. Sometimes both of these rules get broken—even in the same week. It's okay to break the rules, but boundaries also give freedom. They put you and your husband on the same page about what works for your family without unrealistic expectations for each other. Boundaries also give you the freedom to say no when necessary. Just like in parenthood, it's easier to make the rule the bad guy than to feel like you have to disappoint your friend.

No matter how you prioritize certain friendships, there will be times when they take a backseat to the needs of your babies. No matter how well your hobbies fit with goals or core values, there will be days, weeks, and even months that simply don't allow time for them. When our relationships and hobbies become a needy expectation instead of good desire, the sins of selfishness and laziness sneak into the heart.

From Exhaustion to Laziness

Rest turns into laziness when the desire for comfort trumps the desire for God. This is an especially big pitfall for moms who are home with their children. Stay-at-home moms must be vigilant not to take a lack of accountability for their time for granted. All moms need specific moments of rest throughout their workday, but not in every stolen moment. Instead, be overly intentional about specifying moments of rest so you're not tempted to simply rest at every opportunity.

I boost my productivity throughout the day by taking a lunch break. On most days, I eat two lunches. First, I eat a small lunch with my children. Then once my babies are both down for their afternoon nap, my oldest watches a TV show while I eat another small lunch. I let myself do whatever I want during this break: check social media, read a book or blog, listen to a podcast, page through a magazine, anything! This is my moment. It energizes me for the work of caring for my children and managing our household. If I don't have a little time like this scheduled, I elevate the importance of my hobbies or social life to a need instead of a desire, and I tend to choose them over the needs of my children or household.

Laziness is a consistent pattern of choosing the desires of

self over the needs of your job. Proverbs 13:4 says, **The soul of the sluggard craves and gets nothing, while the soul of the diligent is richly supplied.** The more you give in to unscheduled and purposeless free time, the more you want it. It's kind of like Diet Coke; the sugar substitute leaves your body thirsty for more. You drink and drink and never feel satisfied. When I allow myself too much brainless free time instead of a purposeful hobby or working hard at my job of mothering and housekeeping, I find myself wanting more and more "me time."

Let's be diligent in our God-given tasks and have our soul needs richly supplied by the Giver of all good things, not by frivolous free time.

Entitlement Makes Life All about Us

Entitlement has become so pervasive in our society that it has rewritten how even Christians view blessing.

My husband and I got married in a whirlwind of weddings. It was 2007 and home prices were plummeting. Most of our friends who married that year immediately bought houses, but God had us on a different path. We moved across the country as my friends settled down in my home state. God brought us back home a year later, but we lived a transient life of apartments and even my in-laws' basement as we waited for the right time for us to buy.

After a year searching for the right house, we were floored

by the blessing God had for us. It was our dream house at our dream price. I can't tell you how many times a friend would walk in and say something like, "Wow! You lived in tiny apartments and waited for God's timing, and look what he gave you. You totally deserve this."

It was so tempting to buy into the lie they were perpetuating. But we weren't entitled to our dream house no matter how much we sacrificed. It was all grace—an abundant blessing to an unworthy couple. Unfortunately, the entitlement culture we live in has infiltrated Christian thinking.

Entitlement is a sin because it denies the power of the gospel. Our culture believes we are entitled to blessing based on our good works, but the Bible disagrees. God's Word says that we're sinners and that **the wages of sin is death** (Romans 5:8). Far from deserving blessing, without Christ we are **by nature children of wrath** (Ephesians 2:3).

Here's the gospel: Instead of giving us what we deserve, Jesus laid down his life so we could receive **grace upon grace** (John 1:16). The good news is that we deserved only God's wrath and immediate death for our abundance of sin but Jesus died so we can receive endless grace to cover all our past, present, and future sins. The blessing and grace we receive is a result of Jesus' sacrifice, not any small sacrifices we make in this world. We don't deserve any goodness in this life, and we certainly don't deserve the joy of God's presence that we will receive in the next life—but in Christ, we get them!

Let's apply this to motherhood. Our culture perpetuates the lie that what we do dictates what we deserve. Mothers may work harder and serve others more, but we still don't measure up to God's standards of perfection, which means we still deserve death. All our endless working hours and constant self-sacrifices will never be enough to deserve a massage or a relaxing time with friends or an hour alone to read. We may get all those things, but not because we deserve them; it's because our loving God lavishes his grace on the undeserving.

Every good and perfect gift—like stolen moments to do things that bring us delight and rest or sweet fellowship with other women—flows directly from God's fountain of love. This flips our attitude on its head. We are no longer entitled to our free time; instead we rejoice in God's tender propensity to give us good gifts with abundance. Stop your heart from pursuing free time out of a sense of entitlement and start receiving it as a gift of rest from the Creator who knows your real needs better than you do.

Dear Running-on-Empty Mommy, free time won't fill you up. Forgo naming it as a need and start receiving it as a blessing. Renounce laziness and embrace your daily tasks as worship. Use your free moments to pursue meaningful hobbies or build strong friendships. Discover real rest in the One who restores your broken soul to wholeness.

An Unsupermommy's Imperfect Plan

1. Choose hobbies that build your mind, body, and spirit through worshipful work.

2. Save some free time for friendships.

3. Reject laziness and discard me-minded entitlement to receive the blessing of God's propensity to give us more than we ever ask or imagine.

Releasing Expectations for Your Purpose in Life

I spent all of my twenty-six years before I became a mother as a student of myself. I devoted endless hours to dreaming up my desires and making plans to achieve them. I identified my needs and spent my energy meeting them. I had a lot of time to think about me: my relationships, my body, my dreams, my family, my future, my meaning, my career, my personality, and even my purpose.

Then I had my first child. It was like that tiny baby came with a huge eraser. His needs and desires burst onto the scene of my life and erased all those endless hours to think about me. Suddenly my life didn't—*couldn't*—revolve around me. His very life depended upon me putting him first. It was a painful shift. My understanding of who I was and my purpose in life came through my roles and relationships, and this one little baby managed to change every facet of my existence.

Before motherhood, the major reorganizations of my

life—like finishing school, marriage, and changing careers—only affected a few pieces of who I was as a person. Becoming a mom changed everything: my marriage, my career, how I related to my extended family, my body image, my free time, and my friendships. It even changed my spiritual life. That helpless, hungry baby changed every single part of me. Even though I had spent all those countless hours as a student of myself, I only knew myself in relationship to the people and circumstances around me.

As motherhood rerouted my life, God taught me that who I am doesn't depend on my circumstances or my relationships. My body, my mind, and my personality were made by the Creator of the universe, and his relationship to me is the only right way to define myself. I thought I knew myself before motherhood, but it took stripping away the layers of others to find myself in God alone.

I'm sure you've heard people proclaim that motherhood is a noble calling or that mothers have the most important job in the world. Christians often recite that raising godly children has inherent purpose and meaning, implying a mother doesn't need anything beyond that calling. I have to be real with you: These platitudes always feel empty to me.

If my purpose as a godly woman is to raise godly children, what happens when my children are grown? Do I lie down on my couch, put my feet up, and say I've completed the job God gave me? What happens if despite the countless hours memorizing Bible verses, teaching God's grace, and praying for their souls, some of my children don't accept God's gift of salvation? Did I fail as a mom? If my purpose is to raise godly children and that doesn't happen, what did all those countless hours of endless sacrifice amount to? Where did all my meaning and purpose go?

I grew up thinking my purpose was tied up in who I impacted for God, but I had it all wrong. Revealing God to others isn't the purpose of my life; it's the product. My ultimate purpose isn't to love my children or even my husband—it is to love God. "'You shall love the Lord your God with all your heart and with all your soul and with all your mind.' This is the great and first commandment" (Matthew 22:37–38).

My true purpose is first and foremost to love God more. This means that motherhood can't be my ultimate purpose. Godly motherhood is a product of fulfilling my purpose: loving God more by knowing him better. God's purpose for every relationship I have and every circumstance of my life, even one as world shifting as motherhood, is to bring me further up and further in.

Jennie Allen, the founder of IF: Gathering, explains, "No unique purpose for your life will fill your soul. The only thing that will fulfill and settle your soul is God himself."[1]

Motherhood isn't meant to give me life; it's meant to point me to the true Life Giver. Here's the process: God draws me closer to him through difficult circumstances. I grow to know him and love him more. I'm sanctified through a deepening relationship with Christ. Finally, others see Christ in me and God uses that impact how he wills.

The Westminster Catechism says the chief end of man is to glorify God and enjoy him forever.[2] We can't glorify him if we don't know him and love him more than all the other loves in our lives. Motherhood is one part of an endless pursuit to be near to God. Both the trials and the tasks of motherhood are meant to draw us nearer than we've ever been before. Resting in God's power to propel us through our daily rhythms deepens our love for God, sanctifies us, and brings glory to him instead of ourselves. Dependence on God draws us deeper with God.

Therefore, we don't wrap our purpose up in our children—or in any other relationship. Roles and relationships don't define who we are and why we're here. Only one relationship defines us: our relationship with God.

Brad Bigney states, "When it becomes identity, it's almost always idolatry."[3] If we tie up all of who we are in godly motherhood, we establish our children as the focus of our lives instead of God. Then who we are as women becomes dependent upon the achievements, obedience, and godliness of our children. Dear Mommies, we're so much more than the summation of our children. Our purpose lies in the process of becoming more of who we are: Christ carriers.

We're made in the image of God. Theologian Wayne Grudem says, "The fact that man is in the image of God means that man is like God and represents God."[4] Through Christ's work on the cross, we have the opportunity to become more like God and in turn become better representatives of God to those around us. Changing the world or the people around us isn't the purpose of our lives; it's the *result* of our purpose. Becoming Christlike is the goal, and it makes us better representatives of Jesus to everyone in our influence. Finding our identity in what we do is foolishness. Our task of mothering is only effective as the result of who we are in Christ: accepted, forgiven, and loved beyond all human comprehension.

The Purpose of the Mundane

When I was in college, I spent a semester traveling around Great Britain with twenty-five students and two professors from my college's English department. A few days into our trip, my eight-year-old cousin was hit by a car while riding her bike and died. I was trapped on the other side of the world, alone in my mourning with a group of people who didn't know her, but God saw my needs.

He built my relationships with four other women on my trip, one who had lost a sister as a teenager. Those women walked alongside me as I struggled with the purpose of traveling during tragedy. I spent almost one hundred days doing nearly every moment of life with those women. We bonded through mountaintop moments and unexpected tears, but it was the simple meals, quiet walks, endless reading, and silly games that cemented us together. Even now, those women remain an active part of my life.

My relationship with God develops in the same way. It requires both the dramatic, life-changing moments and the ordinary smallness of the everyday to grow roots down deep. Togetherness in the undramatic moments of life builds an abiding trust in God's faithfulness that is essential to weather the stormy days of motherhood. Mundane mommy moments may feel unimportant, but they are our spiritual training grounds.

I have a list of simple tasks to complete every day— whether I want to or not —but my response to the necessary and mundane is the determiner of its value. If I'm annoyed and inconvenienced or do it in my own pride and power, then the act gets washed into the sea of those unseen moments. If I work with joy, as an act of service not just to my child or my husband but to God, the simple moment is suddenly sacred. Worship transforms the pointless into the purposeful.

God is sovereign over the earth-shaking and life-changing, but he is also sovereign over dirty diapers and cluster feeding. When we joyfully accept our jobs and rely on his grace to do them, God is glorified and we are sanctified. No one (including my babies) will ever know or care about the number of diapers I've changed, the noses I've wiped, the medicine I've distributed, the dishes I've done … except God. He gave me each one of those jobs. When I respond in joyful obedience, that is an act of worship.

In her book *Restless*, Jennie Allen writes, "So if we know no place, no job, no marriage, no child is going to fulfill us perfectly, we can make the choice to quit fighting for happiness in all of it and start to fight for God's glory in it."[5] When I start to fight for God's glory in the mundane, true worship pours forth and transforms the meaningless into the momentous.

Motherhood's simplest moments are made meaningful when we set our minds on the Spirit. For to set the mind on the flesh is death, but to set the mind on the Spirit is life and peace (Romans 8:6). I know I can always use more life and peace while changing dirty diapers or disciplining my toddler. The gospel offers us a heart filled with peace and purpose that isn't dependent upon life's circumstances. Amazing grace!

Heather MacFadyen of *God-Centered Mom* blog says, "If my grip is so tight on achieving perfect, my hand is not open to receiving joy."[6] An unsupermommy is a woman holding her plans in open trustful arms before God and expecting God's power to display itself through her weakness. Ordinary tasks completed through God's superpower become moments to give worship and receive joy.

Motherhood isn't a means to fulfilling our need for purpose, but an outpouring of living full of the Spirit. The secret to finding your purpose is simply finding more of God. Knowing and loving God more is the purpose that will never fail us. Each joyful triumph, painful trial, and predictable chore serves one purpose—glorifying God by receiving more of him.

Dear Searching Mommy, your kids may take the bulk of your time, but the bulk of your heart must belong to God. Loving God is your purpose. Your purpose isn't to change the world, raise godly children, or be the best daughter, friend, or wife. Those things are all results. The real purpose in every moment of your life is to root God deeper into the soil of your soul. Then you will blossom into a new creation as the waters of the Holy Spirit feed new growth. Your renewed heart will know Jesus Christ, and him crucified, so deeply that you can't help but see and proclaim his gospel in every moment of your life to everyone around you.

An Unsupermommy's Imperfect Plan

1. Stop searching for purpose in your relationships and circumstances.

2. Experience the only fulfilling and unchanging purpose for your life: knowing and loving God more.

3. Let the purpose of knowing God more transform the mundane into the meaningful.

Embracing Imperfection: Step 3-Charge Up

One of my little guys has been learning the alphabet through osmosis. His older brother is busy with identifying letters, so he has started to pick them up. He doesn't really know them; he *thinks* he knows them. Oh my, that boy is confident in his inaccuracies.

The biggest problem is the letter O. He's so positive that it's called W. We were looking through a book the other day, and he noticed an O. His sausage finger poked at it repeatedly as he proclaimed, "W!"

"That's an O," I corrected.

"W, W, W!"

"Not W. This is the letter O," I tried again.

"No O. Dubba-yooouuu," he articulated slowly for my benefit.

"Let's just move on." I gave up and started to turn the page, but he stopped me.

"It's W, Mommy." He wouldn't allow us to agree to

disagree. He insisted that I identify that O as a W before we could continue.

I cringed inside. I'd love to tell you that I took this moment to explain to him that sometimes we think we're right, but a higher authority tells us we're wrong. Sometimes we're dead certain we can correctly identify what is right in front of us, but God knows the truth. I wish I could say I was that kind of mom in that kind of moment, but I was hungry and just needed him to take his nap so I could eat my lunch.

"Fine. W," I grunted through clenched teeth.

Living Like an Unsupermommy Looks All Wrong

Plugging in to God instead of your own power is downright countercultural. Women are supposed to be empowered by their own abilities. Our strength comes from our independence and confidence. When we can't live by our own power, we feel like failures. God wants us to recategorize our W's to O's by correctly identifying him as our power source.

But God chose what is foolish in the world to shame the wise; God chose what is weak in the world to shame the strong (1 Corinthians 1:27). God likes to use the unexpected—the small and the imperfect—to reflect the grandeur of his glory. He sent Jesus to be born in a manger. He chose Moses, the outcast Israelite, to lead his people to freedom. He made fishermen his intimate companions. He selected Paul, the Christian hater, to become the gospel spreader. If you feel weak, imperfect, and unimportant, you're just the kind of person God wants to use as a vessel for displaying his power to the world.

The normal path of motherhood is to try to be a super-mommy, but God flips it around. He creates strength from weakness. He redeems the imperfect. We might be certain that our struggles of motherhood are failures, but we are calling an O a W. God knows being weak and imperfect gives us access to his grace and power. He's trying to tell us that it's an O, but we have to first accept that it's not a W.

Let's stop calling our weakness failure. Let's start seeing it through God's perspective—a step in the process of receiving his grace and living in his strength. This acceptance is the process of charging up. If you're maintaining a connection to God through abiding, charging up is a direct result. Charging up is humbly accepting his saving and sustaining grace.

We Have to Admit When We're Wrong

Admitting that the letter we always thought was called W is really an O takes a heavy dose of humility. Let me raise my hand and admit to you: I love to be right. I hate realizing I'm not. I spent my first years as a mom trying to be perfect. I wasn't trying to do everything, instead focusing on just a few things I wanted to be good at as a mom. I put all my energy into being a spiritual, academic, and fun mom … and all my energy wasn't enough.

When I realized that my strength only added up to weakness and stopped trying to force God to label my O as a W, I found the truth. I had been wrong about motherhood. The path of motherhood isn't meeting a system of standards to raise the perfect child; it is my whole tired, imperfect heart relying on my infinitely mighty and righteous God.

I finally accepted the humble truth: I'm not enough, but God's grace is. This is the gospel. This unsupermommy method of motherhood works because it simply follows the path God laid out in the gospel. First, we will always be imperfect and will never be enough. Second, Jesus stands in the gap, covering our sin and shame. Next, God uses the imperfect to display his power to those around us. As mothers, this looks like realizing our sinful hearts and tired bodies will always hinder perfect motherhood. We have two choices, to keep hustling and striving to make motherhood work in our own merit or to give up on measuring up and rest in God's grace over our imperfection and weakness.

We'll get to the last step of displaying God's power in a few chapters. For now, let's focus on charging up on God's grace. Grace is a two-fold promise—it saves us and it sustains us.

His Grace Continually Saves Us from Ourselves

Sin is a weakness we can't escape in this life. **For all have sinned and fall short of the glory of God** (Romans 3:23).

This isn't a hopeless truth; it simply represents our need for God's grace. God didn't just extend grace as a one-time act to cover the sins we committed before accepting Jesus' sacrifice. He also extends grace every time we sin after our salvation.

Once we're confronted with the humbling reality that we don't just sin before salvation but continue to sin every day, it's easy to fall into the pit of sin obsession. Some may lay in wait for daily failures or go on sin crusades in their own hearts, living in a constant state of condemnation. But the purpose of salvation is to call us out of sin to live in the freedom of saving grace. **There is therefore now no condemnation for those who are in Christ Jesus** (Romans 8:1).

Yesterday, today, and every future day, God looks upon us and sees Jesus' perfection instead of our failings. Paul David Tripp says, "It is simply a denial of the amazing grace of the gospel of Jesus Christ to treat yourself as an unworthy, impure, and incapable spiritual worm. ... What you and I must meditate on every day is the absolute perfection and completeness of the work of the Lord Jesus Christ."[1]

True humility is recognizing not just that you did and do sin, but also that Jesus' saving work covers all of it. Every moment of every day, grace is bigger than your sin. You may be imperfect in practice, but you stand before God forgiven and freed. If we stay connected to God, our focus will naturally fall to both his greatness and goodness. If we know moment-by-moment a God who continually forgives and endlessly loves, we will be charged up with the freedom that Christ bought for us rather than wallowing in the shame of our imperfection.

Charging up with God's superpower requires recognizing your inability to power yourself in motherhood, holiness, and receiving the grace God offers. He promises this: "And I will give you a new heart, and a new spirit I will put within you. And I will remove the heart of stone from your flesh and give you a heart of flesh. And I will put a new Spirit within you, and cause you to walk in my statutes and be careful to obey my rules" (Ezekiel 36:26–27).

You can't change your heart in your own power, but God's grace has the superpower to replace stony resistance with soft submission. John Piper explains, "Grace is not simply leniency when we have sinned. Grace is the enabling gift of God not to sin. Grace is power, not just pardon."[2]

Accept your imperfection and allow God to save you every day. Charge up with his grace to save you from your own sin-filled heart. His grace grants you peace for past mistakes and hope in God's future redemption.

His Grace Powers Us through Our Weakness

Let's throw out the old Christian saying that God doesn't give us anything we can't handle. In fact, God has a habit of giving us all kinds of things we can't handle on our own. He wants to push us past our own power to complete reliance upon his. Admitting weakness is essential to receiving God's superpower.

Pastor Jason Meyer explains, "Paul gladly boasts in weakness because his real goal is for the power of Christ to rest upon him. He is well pleased with weakness because he knows that when he is weak, he is strong in Christ's strength. … Paul is pleased with being a weak canvas because weak canvases are the only ones that Christ will paint upon."[3] May we allow our imperfect motherhood to be the canvas covered in God's beautiful grace that our children get the blessing to look at every day.

God's saving grace releases us from condemnation for our past, present, and future sin. God's sustaining grace empowers us for every day. After we connect to God, his grace is the supernatural power charged up in us that gives us the energy to do his calling. It's what the Bible is talking about when it says, **His divine power has granted to us all things that pertain to life and godliness** (2 Peter 1:3).

On those days when you need to safety pin your eyes open, God keeps you going. When your teething baby won't stop that fingernails-on-a-chalkboard screaming, God quiets your heart. During the midnight feeding when your baby refuses both the breast and bottle, God is your wisdom. When you feel the isolation of your imperfection, God redeems you. God's grace is abundant in your most empty moments. Stop focusing on your failure and hold desperately to God's grace.

God's Purpose in This Backward Way of Charging Us Up

Acceptance of imperfection looks like foolishness to the world. But admitting that we can't live up to supermommy expectations is actually our ticket to God's superpowers. Instead of us leaving us to our own insufficient power, God converts Jesus' powerful sacrifice into our wisdom and our righteousness and sanctification and redemption (1 Corinthians 1:30). Why? Let the one who boasts, boast in the Lord (v. 31).

When we connect to Jesus and allow the Holy Spirit to charge us up with his powerful grace, it changes us. Just like when we find the perfect baby gadget, we can't stop talking about it. God's work through our weakness drives us to proclaim his greatness to others. It makes us ambassadors for this crazy-backward path toward freedom. We still have moments of fear, exhaustion, anger, and self-centeredness, but the power of God remains bigger than those shortcomings.

Dear Half-Filled Mommy, it's time to exchange good motherhood for gospel motherhood. Apply the truth of the gospel to your everyday imperfections: you're a flawed woman, saved by the Perfect Redeemer, called to showcase his grace through your weak vessel. Your greatest priority is staying connected to his endless superpower. All it takes to charge up with his power is humble acceptance of his saving and sustaining grace. Finally, you will become an electrified conduit of God's superpowers, igniting a display of his glory for those around you.

An Unsupermommy's Imperfect Plan

1. Charging up with God's power means humbly admitting that God's path for success may look like foolishness in our world.

2. Jesus' work of salvation rescues us from all past sins and future failures. It offers us freedom in Christ's saving grace instead of bondage to perfection.

3. When we live by God's superpowers instead of our insufficient internal energy, God gets all the glory and we get all the good!

Releasing Expectations for a Superdaddy

You know by now that I had abundant expectations for my baby and myself. I doubt you're surprised to hear that I also had a plan for my husband.

First of all, when our baby was born, he would take a week off from work and work from home for a second week. Once he did return to the workforce, he would check in several times a day to hear all the cute moments he'd missed (because the baby was bound to be one cuddly bundle of never-ending cuteness!). When he came home, he would rescue the baby from my arms so I could nap as he prepared our favorite meal and tidied up around the kitchen. Weekends would be filled with neighborhood walks and city festivals, our baby wrapped proudly to his chest. Yep, I expected a superdaddy.

My first four months as a mom were beyond survival mode—more like complete panic. I was so focused on my baby that I couldn't meet my own physical and emotional needs. My dear husband fell through the cracks of my emotional exhaustion. I honestly didn't see how much he was drowning in daddyhood until our relationship started imploding.

Fellow mommies, in the face of overwhelming expectations, we can't forget our husbands. A healthy relationship can survive a few weeks of distraction, but soon our focus has to fall back to mutual encouragement or we will lose the happy dependence that makes marriage beautiful.

Ironically, I blamed my husband for not adjusting to fatherhood when I was miserable myself. We were both in the trenches, but we weren't holding hands and working side by side. Instead of resting in God's sufficiency, I expected my husband to be my savior. I anticipated an emotional and physical piggyback ride through the worst of it. My husband tried to tell me that his own legs were broken, but I ignored him. I assumed that with a superdaddy beside me, motherhood would magically become easy. I looked to my imperfect husband for strength instead of leaning on my super-powered God.

I wish I had taken the time to empathize with his struggle, but instead I told myself that my pain trumped his. I compared the difficulty of our new roles, and his looked easy-peasy. There's a lot of grumbling these days about the lack of postpartum care for new mothers—and it's a legitimate concern—but let's not forget the dads struggling with postpartum adjustment. The last thing our struggling husbands need is for us to expect them to be savior-style superdaddies.

From My Man's Mouth

When I sat down to write this chapter, I finally took the time to listen to my husband's story. As he shared, three major struggles emerged: loss of control, loss of relationship with his wife, and physical demands.

I played a role in at least two of those problems. I wasn't surprised to hear that Wes felt exhausted during his transition to fatherhood. I ignored how physically taxing it was for him to pick up my slack in the housekeeping department. I don't think it's because he was a man (men can be great at household chores); the extra housework was just one thing too much between the added pressure of a difficult baby, an emotional wife, and a regular job.

It wasn't wrong for me to ask for his help, but I didn't really *need* everything I asked him to do. I had the audacity to turn down meal support from my church, yet I expected my husband to cook. What was I thinking? Accept every meal you're offered, eat with paper and plastic, let the dirt pile up on the floors, and just let life be. Taking care of your baby is enough. Bonding with your baby is enough. Processing your new life together is enough. You don't need housework expectations for yourself or your husband on top of it. Let all the extras go and just live. You won't regret it.

On top of the increased physical demands of housework and lack of sleep, my husband missed me. He tried to tell me this, but his desire for a more physical, emotional, and spiritual connection fueled a growing resentment that he didn't understand the pressure I felt. I thought I didn't have any more to give. I had forgotten one of marriage's beautiful truths: an investment in my husband always pays dividends back to me.

You may feel emotionally bankrupt, but if you put your last penny into your marriage, you're investing in yourself too. God made you one flesh; take care of your husband's needs with the same fervor you give your own. You will both benefit. My husband's number one piece of advice for new moms is to set time aside for the kind of rest that includes relationship building for the two of you, especially conversation. Dear Mommies, if our husbands' needs are really so simple, I think we can manage that.

My husband's hardest adjustment was the loss of control over his free time. We couldn't go to a movie. It was no longer simple to go out to dinner. He usually spent time on the weekend doing his hobbies, but I wanted him at home with me. He understood why I needed him there, but he still resented it. I didn't have much grace for him even though I felt the same struggle. I wanted to be in control of when I slept, when I ate, and what I accomplished, but the whims of my newborn never allowed for that.

It was a wake-up call for both of us. Of course, our previous feeling of control was really only a delusion—ultimately God controls our circumstances no matter how unencumbered—but it hurt to lose the feeling of control. You can't teach your husband this lesson; it's between him and God. I've found the most effective way to nudge my husband toward more of God is to pursue more of God myself. When God is working in your heart, your husband will notice.

My Self-Righteous and Self-Absorbed Expectations

Setting expectations for others rarely results in success. When others don't meet our expectations, our good desires develop into needs. When we look to other people to save us from our circumstances, we're setting them on the throne of our heart instead of God.

My husband and I had countless expectations that the other failed to perform. As we each exalted our expectations into needs, we began to resent the other for not meeting those needs. I expected that my husband would occasionally get up with the baby at night, but he left early for work. He expected that since I was home all day, I would find other time to sleep if I had a rough night. This was just one of many expectations I had for my husband that he failed to meet. When he didn't act how I expected, my desire for his help developed into a self-proclaimed need. When my need wasn't met, I fell into two forms of pride: self-righteousness and self-absorption.

Despite my own failure at meeting my lofty expectations, I couldn't give grace for his. We're all guilty of the sin of self-absorption, because it's a facet of pride. It's part of our inherent sinfulness to constantly think of ourselves. Thinking of others will not cure you of thinking of yourself. Self-absorption isn't just a sin because it ignores the world around you; it's a sin because it ignores God. Being awash in the greatest challenge of your life doesn't give you a free pass to only think of yourself. You must replace thinking of yourself with thinking about God.

When our minds are filled by God, it's impossible to be absorbed with ourselves. If I hadn't lost sight of God, I wouldn't have gotten the mixed-up notion that my husband could meet my needs. He can't save me; God already did that.

God-absorption defeats the sin of self-righteousness toward our husbands too. When my husband didn't meet superdaddy standards, I was prone to sanctimonious inner rants. *A dad's job is so easy. I could do it in my sleep. In fact, imagine all the sleep I would be getting if I was the dad! He can't manage a few hours at home with the baby after being gone at work all day? Fatherhood is so simple. He doesn't know how much work it is to be a mom. There's no comparison, so he'll never understand me.*

Yikes, that's some obviously sinful thinking, but I can't count the number of times I've told those lies to myself. We don't give dads nearly as much grace as we give our fellow moms. We think our experiences don't compare, but that's a lie. Before a righteous God, we all stand on level ground. Repeat the gospel to yourself. Meditate on what God has done for you. He gives us extra helpings of grace as often as we need them. May we rewrite the lies on our hearts with the truth of God's Word, then extend extra helpings of grace to our husbands too.

The lesson of the unsupermommy is to embrace your failures as opportunities for God's power and grace to abound in our lives. Can we apply it to the unsuperdaddies standing beside us?

In Matthew 18, Jesus tells the parable of the unforgiving servant. It's the story of a man who is forgiven of an enormous debt by his king but then goes on to demand payment of a very small debt by his fellow servant. God forgave us of a huge debt, far beyond what we even imagine. Can we forgive our husbands when they fail to live up to superdaddy standards? Can we pass along the heaping extra portions of grace that God so graciously bestows on us?

Practical Ways to Support Your Husband as a Dad

Dads need help just like moms do. To support your husband as a dad, first encourage him to do the things he enjoys about fatherhood. If you don't know what they are, ask him.

When my youngest son was around nine months old, my husband admitted that he loves to put him to bed. I love it too, but he needed those baby snuggles more than I did. The more moments of joy our husbands can capture with our children, the easier the tough patches will be for them. As moms, we can facilitate those moments of joy our husbands might not even recognize they need.

Next, allow him to husband you. My postnatal emotional instability was painful for my husband to watch. He wanted to fix it but didn't know how. It's an age-old problem. As women, we want our husbands to just listen and affirm, but they want to hear and fix. There's no changing God's design for us, but we can give grace. If your husband tries to fix your problem, don't get angry that he isn't listening. Maybe it's time for you to accept the fix.

I can assure you that I certainly didn't want to take my husband's suggestion that we hire someone to clean our home for a while. It felt like admitting defeat and accepting my own ineptitude, but it was really just a matter of humility. I wanted to feel bad about how I didn't have the time or energy to do it. When I finally humbled my heart, I saw the wisdom and love in what he was suggesting. Sometimes as women we need to allow some duct tape on our lives instead of wallowing in our misery. The duct tape might not fix it perfectly, but if it can make it better, let's accept the help.

Finally, assume the best intentions. Don't take your husband's every action as a personal offense against you or your children. When he makes a suggestion for improvement, it doesn't mean he thinks you're a bad mom or you're raising bad kids. Assume that he means the best, even if what he said or did was hurtful. Seek to restore relationship, but don't accuse. Ask him why he did or said it, then believe him. Because you love him, trust him.

Dear Unsupermommies, our husbands may not be perfect, but they're part of God's perfect plan for our lives. May we seek God's salvation first, then pass along the grace he gives us to our husbands.

An Unsupermommy's Imperfect Plan

1. Don't expect your husband to save you from motherhood.

2. Make allowances for yourself and your husband for an imperfect home as you adjust to the pattern of your newborn.

3. Fill your heart with the truth of God's grace, so there is no longer any room for self-absorption and self-righteousness.

Releasing Expectations for Parenting Together

When my first baby was born, I didn't just become a mother. I became one member of a pair of parents. Not just a mom figuring it out on her own, but a partner with my husband in this child-rearing adventure.

Honestly, sometimes I tell myself it would be easier to do on my own. I'm the kind of confident person who thinks her opinion is always right. When it comes to my babies, I'm sure I know best. I know I've admitted that I worry about following the standards of the other moms around me. I feel inadequate in my abilities as I scroll through the feeds of supermommies on Instagram. I call my mom for advice all the time. But when it comes to my husband? Well, he's not home all day with the kids like I am. He doesn't know the babies like I do. Suddenly I'm certain that I'm doing all the right things.

When he wants to try a different method with one of the children, I feel like a failure. I tell myself he doesn't trust me, that he thinks I'm incapable. I'm sure you're not surprised to hear that I really care about his opinion of me as a parent. I want him to see me as the perfect mother. On the other hand, I want him to lead our family in the right direction, but every time he suggests a trajectory, I see it as a personal attack on my plans.

I care what my husband thinks about me—a lot. I also need his help—a lot. I'm still learning how to parent well with him. This isn't an area I have all figured out. As I write this, I can see what needs to happen: more communication and more trust.

Parenting Is an Outpouring of Our Imperfect Love

Parenting involves meeting the physical needs of our children, giving them spiritual, emotional, intellectual, and social instruction, and providing discipline. Love is *how* we do all those things. In theory, we always love our children, but practice can be so much more difficult. Good parenting requires more than our failing human love; it needs God's love filling us up and flowing out through us. Our imperfect human love will only get us so far.

There will be days we don't love our children enough to spend our mealtimes focused on feeding them without grumbling. Sometimes we won't love them enough to watch for moments to point them to God instead of watching our social media feeds. There will be days when we throw in the towel on good discipline because their constant disobedience drives us over the edge of anger. There will always be days of imperfect parenting when we trust in our own love for our babies and it's just not enough. That's why God's love, moving through our imperfect hands, must be the battery that powers all the other parts of parenting.

God made each of us as different kinds of conduits for his love. People simply love differently than each other. Your husband's love for your children as he meets their needs, instructs them, and disciplines them will likely look different from yours. Each person on the parenting team has a different role, but you should both be working toward the same goal.

We can't just do parenting together; we also need to talk parenting together. The best way to get on the same page as parents is to actually talk about it. Make plans and goals for your family, then gently remind each other of those goals as you parent. Some days one or both of you will fail. That's normal. If we never failed, we wouldn't need grace. Accept God's saving grace for your own imperfection, and extend forgiving grace for your husband's imperfect moments too.

Talk about how to find a new path to achieve your parenting goals for your kids. All good plans get adapted. When you begin, you don't know what your baby will be like, and you don't even know what you'll be like as a mom and what your husband will be like as a dad. New roles take time to understand. It's essential to discuss how you want to do these things, then expect that even if you're on the same page, your actions will probably look different from each other. Your parenting doesn't need to be exactly the same to be accomplishing the same goal. Know your plans, and give each other freedom within them.

When you talk with your husband about parenting, be open and forgiving. It's easy to go into parenting conversations in full attack mode. Don't start parenting conversations certain of your own correctness and armed with proof to win the argument. Instead, remember your own insecurities, the days you feel like nothing you do as a mom works right. Recall the moments when you're scared because you can't seem to stop making mistakes. Remembering how much grace you require will help you extend grace for your husband's failures and insecurities.

An attack will lead him to either fight against you or flee in self-condemnation. Instead, come in a spirit of humility, remembering that no one is perfect here. Get on the same team. Figure it out together. What's the goal? How will being a conduit for God's love to your baby look for you? How will it look for your husband? You may think your way of loving is the right way, but God gave that baby to both of you for a reason. Be open about your concerns, be honest about your insecurities, and let the words flow in love to each other.

It's easy to figure out your perfect plan for parenting

together when the baby is sleeping and the house is peaceful. It's harder while living together in the thick of it. One way to keep on the same page daily is what I call a status report. When I disagree with my husband on the way he is parenting, I find myself thinking, *Well, he doesn't know what he is doing because I'm the one at home all day with the child.*

Here's the rub: If he doesn't have all the information he needs to parent our boys well, that's on me. The only way to fix his lack of knowledge is by doing a status report daily before he comes home or as soon he gets here. Generally, my husband is able to call me and check in at lunchtime. I can give him a ministatus report then, letting him know how each boy is doing that day and where we're struggling and also where we're succeeding. We also try to do a check-in when he is driving home.

When we miss our status report time, all of us suffer. My husband comes home and has no idea what he is walking into with the kids. He immediately goes on the offensive, trying to care for our children through both love and discipline, but he doesn't really know the background of our day if I don't take the time for that status report. It's my responsibility to equip my husband by giving him knowledge. If it doesn't happen on his drive home, I must tear my attention away from dinner to get him up to speed as soon as he gets home. It only takes a few minutes, but how often I fail to do it.

Let's prepare our husbands to parent well by keeping them informed. Let's share with our husbands the tricks that worked for us that day and the places we're struggling, then trust them as parents.

Trust Your Husband

When you married your man, you covenanted with him in trust. You linked your life directly to his. Maybe his ideas for your children are totally different from yours. Maybe your goals are the same but your paths go in opposite directions. Trust him and respect him. Outline a plan for how each of you will proceed in parenting together, then don't undermine it when he is gone.

As moms, it's easy to control all of the parenting by default. We simply have more time with our children. Even if you're a mom who works, you probably log more hours of direct care with your children than your husband does. Agreeing in word but doing your own thing in action will tear apart the trust your husband has placed in you. So talk, talk, talk until you find a way to come together, then support it in action.

As parents, we set plans and goals for our children, but God determines their steps. Ultimately, all our parenting decisions, significant or trivial, fall under God's sovereignty. God chose both you and your husband to raise that baby. Don't believe in yourselves or your best laid plans, but trust in God's power to work through you.

Dear Inconsistent Mommy, God loves your babies even more than you do. Hold your children in open arms before God. They are safe in his sovereign grace. He loves them the most. He has proven himself faithful. Trust him.

An Unsupermommy's Imperfect Plan

1. Partner in a plan for parenting, remembering that each of you will probably implement the plan differently based upon your personality.

2. Trust your husband. You chose to covenant with him in marriage, and God chose both of you to raise your child together.

3. When all your parenting feels painfully imperfect, trust God.

Releasing Expectations for Your Marriage

It's not pretty to admit, but every time I have a new baby, my marriage struggles. As Jim Gaffigan says, "Imagine you're drowning, then someone hands you a baby."[1] Babies make it nearly impossible to meet even our most essential human needs, like food and sleep. Hunger and exhaustion breed emotional overreactions. Most days I wouldn't be upset if my husband started texting someone while I was talking to him, but in the early baby days, I wanted to toss his phone in the toilet.

How could he be so inconsiderate? Doesn't he understand that I need his attention? When my essential needs aren't met, I get, well, *really needy*. I've admitted that I've expected a lot of my husband post-baby. No one could meet the expectations I had for him. Add his unmet needs to my crazy hormones and we've got a recipe for marriage disaster. There was only one way to rescue our marriage in the face of a double dose of neediness and expectations—find God first.

Strengthen Your Marriage by Rekindling Your First Love

I'm not great at hair. I'm all thumbs. Actually, that's too nice of a description. I'm all useless pinky fingers. I inherited the ten-pinky-finger problem from my mom, so as a little girl I was lucky to beg braids off my BFF's older sister whenever I got the chance. Sometimes when I got really desperate, I would try a braid on myself, but the best I could manage was a twist. Hair binder at the top, then two sections of hair simply twisted together.

But the twist came with an inherent problem: it wasn't strong. As the day passed by, it would unravel. Two cords simply aren't strong enough when there's nothing locking them together.

Marriage can't be a twist. It has to be a braid. **A threefold cord is not quickly broken** (Ecclesiastes 4:12). Sin creates a frailty in our relationships. When two people get twisted up together in marriage, sin is the gravity slowly forcing them apart. Marriages require the third strand of Jesus to bind the two people together. Because of this phenomenon, we must cling to our God before we can rebuild our marriage.

Expecting marriage to meet our needs is the most common way we sabotage our marriages. Only a relationship with the living God can satisfy our innate hunger for love and acceptance. Here's something to really make your head spin: Satisfaction isn't really the goal. Jesus is the goal. Satisfaction, love, and acceptance are just bits of grace sprinkled on top of the true prize: Jesus himself. Emmanuel—God with us.

It's a little like dating. Ideally, the goal of dating isn't to receive the security that comes with marriage, but to know the man. In the same way, the goal of salvation isn't earthly satisfaction or even heaven, but experiencing a real and vibrant relationship with the God of the universe in this world and the one to come.

Pastor Brad Bigney explains that because every person's heart is a vacuum, it will always be filled with something.[2] Ideally, our hearts are filled with God. However, our wandering hearts often search to be filled by people, possessions, or circumstances—all things that will never satisfy our longing.

Marriage isn't meant to satisfy our longings, but to point us back to God. When you fill the vacuum of your heart with God instead of your marriage, you'll find true contentment. Suddenly a marriage that once felt insufficient becomes a source of secondary satisfaction. You don't need it to fill you up anymore because you're already full. In the same way, you don't go to a five-star restaurant when you've just ran a marathon and need sustenance.

Don't come to the marriage table needy and starving, but for the joy of savoring each taste. If you come hungry, you'll devour the entire experience without enjoying it. Come to the marriage table already satisfied, and everything you get feels like more than enough—like the proverbial icing on top of the cake.

A Steady Diet of the Fruit of the Holy Spirit

The fruit of the Spirit is the best food you can give your marriage. Each moment spent treasuring Jesus above the other valuable things in our lives, like our children and our marriage, builds up the broken strands of our earthly relationships. When we value Jesus highly, the natural response is to want the people we love to know Jesus. When our hearts desire to display Jesus to the people we love, we are less likely to sin against them.

A heart filled with the Spirit flows out in love, joy, peace, patience, kindness, goodness, faithfulness, gentleness, and self-control. If our husbands felt all those good emotions rolling off us instead of grumpiness, exhaustion, anger, frustration, and selfishness, it would be easier to love us. Our men might even wonder what changed in us and where all that fruit was flowing from.

Being filled with the Spirit is contagious. When a husband and wife both catch a feverish filling of the Spirit, their marriage cord grows thick. Trials still come and sin still happens, but the sturdy cord they've built around their personal relationships with Jesus remains strong.

Stop Trying to Fix Your Husband

Sanctification may be the result of marriage, but the job belongs to God. The best way to impact your husband is to start with yourself. You're not in charge of your husband, God is. When your husband sees evidence of the Holy Spirit in your life, he'll want more of it for himself. Remember how I said the fruit of the Spirit makes our marriage stronger? Well, it's also our sanctification toolbox.

If you want to fix your marriage, stop trying to fix your husband. Instead, fix yourself first through the fruit of the Spirit. Replace selfishness with love. Replace discontentment with joy. Replace anxiety with peace. Replace a short temper with patience. Replace criticism with kindness. Replace self-righteousness with goodness. Replace forgetfulness with faithfulness. Replace harsh responses with gentleness. Replace unrestrained desires with self-control. In short, replace sin and legalism with the free abundance of the Holy Spirit. Easier said than done, right?

The abundant fruit of the Spirit doesn't come from our own work, but from staying connected to God and charging up with his power. The fruit of the Spirit is the antithesis of sin—your own sin and also your husband's. If you want to see holiness in your husband's life, let it first abound in yours. When your husband sins, responding with grace that can only be a result of the Spirit is the most effective way to produce change in him.

In the meantime, don't keep lists of your husband's faults. Keep lists of the things you love. Praise them. Enjoy them. Find contentment with the man you have instead of longing for the one you imagine. Encourage him in his pursuit of God. Acknowledge the fruit you see in his life, and find joy in God's great work in his life.

Now It's Time to Get Physical

Yep, I'm talking sex here. Mommies, I get it. Post-baby sex can be difficult. It's hard to find the time and energy to feel in the mood. It can be straight-up uncomfortable or even painful for a while. Our lady parts feel downright asexual after birth and breastfeeding. It usually requires work to make sex feel great again, and there's not much extra energy leftover for that kind of work.

The truth is, God created you as a sexual being. Motherhood may bury that feeling, but it doesn't strip it away completely. It's time to dig for that feeling again. Sex isn't just a good thing for our husbands; it's good for us too. It gives us the pleasure of being one with our husband in a way that nothing else does.

I'm not going to tell you how much you should be having

sex, but I'm telling you that you should be doing it. Stop putting sex at the end of your list. Take a minute to evaluate your current sex life. How often could you have sex with your husband? Got a number? Now add one more time to it. Aim to have sex one more time than you think is logistically possible. As a mom, you will always fall short of your goal. Set the goal a little high and you'll still have sex enough, even when life gets in the way.

Not sure if what's enough for you will be enough for your husband? Ask him. Don't be nervous. Be honest with each other and set a goal that works for both of you.

During those really rough weeks when sex keeps getting pushed to the side for other needs (like more sleep), keep communication open with your husband. Say to him, "I was planning to have sex tonight, but now I'm just so exhausted. Let's plan on tomorrow." This does two things: It tells your husband that you still desire him, and it creates a plan to fix the problem. If you don't say anything, days may turn into weeks before your good intentions finally have the energy to love on him. It's essential to feel wanted by each other even if you're simply too exhausted to act on the desire.

Let's be honest with our husbands—even spell it out for them if we have to. Sometimes men just need that. Let's tell them the things that may be holding us back from wanting physical intimacy. If you need more emotional support beforehand, tell your husband. If you need time away from the baby to crave more intimacy, tell your husband. Spur-of-the-moment passion is few and far between for parents. Now is the time for intentionality. Talk about it, and make goals and plans together.

Take the time to make some plans of your own. If you want to have sex with your husband that night, you don't have to tell him in the morning, but you probably need to tell yourself. Women often require more anticipation to build up passion. You can rework your day to save energy and passion for your nighttime activities. Maybe you'll take a bath instead of doing the dishes. Maybe you'll keep dinner simple or use paper plates. Maybe you'll spend time thinking of what you love about your husband. Know yourself and know your husband, and create an atmosphere that builds passion.

Sex isn't an extravagance; it's an essential. If you feel like a healthy sex life is impossible in this season, let me encourage you. Nine years and three kids later, our sex is better than it has ever been before. It's not as frequent, but it's so much better. What's our secret? We're intentional about getting better at what feels best. We're open about what we like, and we listen to each other's desires. Now go grab your husband and get busy at finding your best. You won't regret it!

Dear Dissatisfied Mommy, if you're aching over your marriage, you're probably focusing on the wrong thing. Shift your focus to God and ask him to change you and your marriage. You're first and foremost the bride of Christ. Find contentment in your relationship with the first love of your life, and let your relationship with your husband be the icing on the cake. Then take the time to enjoy all the emotional, spiritual, and physical benefits of marriage.

The Ugly Truth I Can't Stay Quiet About

Sweet Mommy Friends, there's a problem in the church today that we're too quick to ignore: emotional and physical abuse in marriage. Don't assume your friends and your church are immune to the problem. Statistically speaking, you probably know someone experiencing abuse. Physical abuse is easier to identify, but emotional abuse can lie quietly beneath the surface.

On the Biblical Counseling Coalition's blog, Lily Park identifies emotional abuse by explaining, "Emotional abuse occurs when someone tries to control you through actions or words. They might not physically hurt you, but they know how to instill fear through intimidation and manipulation."[3]

Maybe you know a woman losing herself in the manipulative control of her husband. If you're thinking of someone right now, I suggest you read *Is It My Fault? Hope and Healing for those Suffering Domestic Violence* by Lindsey and Justin Holcomb.[4]

If you're a woman trapped in the abusive cycle of manipulation and control, hear me: You have value. You're adored and cherished by God. Don't keep quiet. You can be loving and submissive to your husband by seeking the help of a counselor or the church to bring him to repentance. Find someone to help you. If the first person you talk to doesn't believe you, search for another.

God sees your pain. He wants you to live in freedom and grace. If you feel alone and lost, know that I'm praying for you. God wants to lead you out of the darkness of abuse and into the light of freedom. Please seek godly help. You can't do this on your own.

An Unsupermommy's Imperfect Plan

1. Expect God's sanctification to bind your marriage together. If you want to change your marriage, start with your own heart.

2. Seek satisfaction in God first, then enjoy marriage as the icing on the cake.

3. Make an intentional plan for physical intimacy.

Embracing Imperfection: Step 4-Ignite with God's Superpower

Dear Mommy, do you feel like you never accomplish anything? Well, give yourself a big ole pat on the back—you have almost accomplished reading an entire book! Only one chapter left. Quick, run into the kitchen and write "Finish a book" on your to-do list, then come back. For once, you're about to cross something off your list!

We've been on a journey together. You've seen a lot of my mess. I hope you've found some solidarity here. Imperfect messes are certainly welcome with me. If you ever meet me, I want you to come give me a hug. If you've read my story, you know me. Although I might not know the intimate details about your babies like you know mine, I care about yours. You, dear Mommy, matter to me. If you need to talk about motherhood or share about your crazy little ones, please reach out. Let's connect online or in person, because I'm just another imperfect mommy like you.

When I started writing this book, I had a four-month-old, a seventeen-month-old, and a three-year-old. As I start this final chapter, my boys are almost two, three, and five. I want you to know that even though I wrote a book while my boys were little, I'm no supermommy. I've been writing this for nearly two years, and, as you can see, it's not an especially long book. It'll be another six months of revisions before this ever hits the shelf.

I don't have a lot of space in my life for writing; these thoughts have been gathered together by frantically typing on my phone as my baby sucked his bottle or as my kids played next to me, compiling them into chapters while a babysitter helped out, and editing them during naptimes at the expense of a clean house or a home-cooked dinner. If you had told me when I had my first baby that I would one day write a book as a mom of three little ones, I would have been proud. I would have thought I'd discovered the super-mommy secret.

And I would have been wrong.

This book only happened because I unplugged from my expectations, embraced imperfection, and connected to God's superpower. This book is physical proof that the humble path of the unsupermommy grants immeasurable strength to a struggling woman living in obedience to God's unexpected plans.

You've read about my battles, and now I want to share a

little victory. God's change in my life has never been so evident. When I found out I was unexpectedly pregnant with my third boy when my second was only five months old, I felt completely defeated. I was already failing, and I couldn't imagine taking on more responsibility and ever being a stable, functioning person again.

This last week, I had a stomach bug. It wasn't the normal puke-your-guts-out for twelve hours and feel better though; it was occasional nausea for over a week. It felt hauntingly similar to my earliest pregnancy symptoms, but I couldn't manage to get all three boys into a store so I could buy a test. On the seventh day, as the sickness was getting worse instead of better, I broke down and asked my husband to buy a test for me on his way home.

In the next year I'm overseeing the building of our new house and getting this book published as my husband starts a new job. It certainly wasn't good timing for a new baby. My reaction should have been the same overwhelming fear of my last unplanned pregnancy but it wasn't. This time I knelt down on my hard kitchen floor and prayed, *God, not my will but yours be done. I know you will grant me all the grace and power to make it through the storm. I can do all this through your faithfulness.*

Adding a baby to an already hectic schedule no longer felt like a death sentence to my sanity, because now I know the depths of God's faithfulness. I know in the deepest places of my soul that God grants me everything I need for life and godliness in any circumstance. Instead of sinking in self-doubt, I fell into his faithfulness.

The test revealed it really was a stomach bug—no unexpected pregnancy here—but I'm glad this happened. It proved to me that this unsupermommy thing works. It changes the heart despite the circumstances. It's freed me from an expectation of easy living. It's developed in me a sound confidence in God's faithfulness. The truth that God's grace is always greater than my trials is rooted deep in my soul. As his great grace lives in me, God's power ignites in me to be free, firm, and overflowing to the world around me.

You Are Free Indeed

God's way isn't the simplest way. The road to heaven is rocky, narrow, and long, but it's the only path of freedom. Humans are born burdened with sin and self, but Christ sets us free. Jesus tells the burdened and weary to come to him: "For my yoke is easy, and my burden is light" (Matthew 11:30).

A yoke is a wooden beam placed on a pulling animal, like an ox or horse, so the master can guide it in the right direction. We like to think we're in control, but the truth is there is always a yoke on us. Sometimes we live under the yoke of our own expectations; our expectations control our actions when we exalt them in our hearts to the level of essential needs instead of hopes and desires submitted to God's sovereignty. When we release our expectations and embrace imperfection to receive more of God, we find freedom in his easy yoke and light burden.

Those words, *easy yoke* and *light burden*, feel self-contradictory. Imagine this: God is a farmer sitting on his wagon. Before him is a heavy yoke of meeting his standards, the law of the Old Testament. He hooks you up to it, and it feels impossible. It weighs more than you can possibly bear. You will fail under its pressure. But suddenly the weight is lifted and the burden is gone. Why? Because next to you stands Jesus, bearing the heavy weight of the burden, making God's driving yoke the one path to freedom from the burden of sin and exalted expectations.

In Christ we receive grace over our imperfections. Freedom to feel joy despite circumstances. Freedom to release our expectations to his sovereign plan. Freedom to live lightly underneath a burden that is shouldered by Christ's perfect sacrifice. "So if the Son sets you free, you will be free indeed" (John 8:36). It's time to stop running, scratching, and hustling our way into the good graces of God and the world. Instead, let's become moms who rest in the freedom of redeemed imperfection.

Stand Firm in His Faithfulness

The trials of motherhood seem simple: a bad night's sleep, a teething child, an explosive blowout, a hungry eater. It's not the stuff of prison camps, but it's hard. It never lets up.

It feels unending and impossible. I'm the first person to say that motherhood is the toughest work I've ever done in my life (and I spent my four college summers doing manual labor). It's physical, visceral work, but it's also emotional and spiritual work.

In fact, the hardest work of motherhood happens in our own hearts. Every day is a battle—will we live for self and accomplish our tasks on our own, or will we submit to God's sovereignty and connect to our only real source of power? This isn't a one-time decision; it's an every morning, sometimes every moment, choice.

Motherhood is a world of circumstances that are beyond our control. Babies are enigmas. In the words of Bono, they move in mysterious ways. We can't control the circumstances of motherhood, but we can control how we respond to them. Paul David Tripp admonishes us to remember "that God's primary goal is not changing our situations or relationships so that we can be happy, but changing us through our situations and relationships so that we will be holy."[1]

Will we fight for our expectations like we need them to live, or will we rest in the truth that Jesus is the only thing we need to survive? Will we fight for our wants, or will we open ourselves to sanctification? If you want your reaction to difficulty to be resting in Jesus, you must stay plugged in and charged up with his grace. It's the only path to experience freedom and stand firm when the gentle waves of an early morning turn into the squalls of a difficult afternoon.

You must remain connected to God and fully charged with his grace, or you won't have enough power to stand firm. Your heart will always default to feelings of inadequacy. Don't worry, Mommy, if you find your mind trudging through the muck of self-doubt, you can reorient it by simply speaking the truth of God's faithfulness despite your imperfection.

Psalm 145 is one of my favorite reorienting Scriptures. Next time you find your heart wandering into lies, read it. Then remember, the sacrifice of Jesus allows us to come back to freedom and God's faithfulness no matter how many times we fail in a day.

God's power is waiting. We just need to connect, charge up, and let it ignite us.

God Gives More Grace Than We Can Need for Ourselves

Connecting to God's grace is like putting a 40-watt bulb into 120 watts of power. It's four D batteries when all we needed for our day is one AAA. What happens with all that excess energy? It overflows from our hearts to ignite the world around us. We call it joy, and it's one of the most delightful results of connecting and charging up.

John Piper defines joy this way: "Christian joy is a good feeling in the soul, produced by the Holy Spirit, as he causes us to see the beauty of Christ in the Word and in the world."[2] Joy is the result of knowing God well. The more we know of God and the gospel, the more beautiful they are to our souls. When we connect to God continually and get filled with the Holy Spirit, we receive joy. Not joy that depends on how easy our baby is. Not joy from achieving all our expectations. But joy that overflows out of a deeper relationship with Jesus, built through the ordinary means of our everyday lives.

There are endless benefits of connecting to God's superpowers and charging up with his grace, but the most infectious is joy. Joy is simply contagious. Joy is the means of God's grace overflowing your cup and extending to others. Our joy from connecting to God has the power to ignite a desire for God in the lives of others.

A joyful mommy makes God look good to everyone in her influence. A mom overflowing with joy charges the atmosphere of her home with God's grace. Her children will see firsthand the freedom and satisfaction of dependence upon God's superpower. They will watch living proof that God's superpower always trumps the world's self-empowerment. This joyful home is available to all who connect to God, charge up on grace, and ignite their lives with God's superpower.

An Unsupermommy's Final Call

Dear Unsupermommy, if your soul aches from the exhaustion of trying to meet supermommy standards, just stop. Give up on measuring up. Let your motherhood be transformed into a beautiful picture of the gospel in your everyday, imperfect moments. All you have to do is unplug from your expectations, embrace imperfection, and connect to God's superpower. May we become a generation of unsupermommies who live freely in their salvation, stand firmly on God's faithfulness, and ignite the world around us with grace-driven joy.

Acknowledgments

First and foremost, *Unsupermommy* comes from God. He deserves all the glory for any of the results of this book. I began as a Moses, and he made me a mouthpiece. When I was reluctant, God was patient and faithful. *Unsupermommy* was simply obedience to his unwavering call.

Wes, you sacrificed personal comforts to make this happen. You never thought this was crazy and always believed when I was overwhelmed. Your love is such a safe place for me, despite all my imperfections. I love you!

Isaac, Zander, and Judah, my dear blessings, you were the instruments of pushing me out of my comfort zone of capable and into the powerful arms of Jesus. I love being your mom. Thank you for giving me grace when I do it so imperfectly.

Mom and Dad, thank you for constantly preaching the truth you learned at Faith Biblical Counseling conferences, especially that I do what I do because I want what I want. Thanks for introducing me to Paul David Tripp and Brad Bigney, whose words transformed my heart and inspired me to submit my mommy desires to God's plan for me.

Beki, Janelle, and Katie, thank you for reading my roughest draft of my first chapters and helping me polish them up to show my publisher. Thank you for your prayers, wise words, unique perspectives, and encouragement.

Ally, you pushed me to trust God when I was afraid of his plan. You always believe God wants to use imperfect me. I love having you in my corner.

The Broadstreet Publishing team, you took my imperfect words and developed them into this tangible book. A special thanks to David Sluka, who recognized the potential of *Unsupermommy* through something as simple as social media. I'm so glad God brought our paths to cross again!

Notes

Chapter 1

1 Paul David Tripp, *New Morning Mercies: A Daily Gospel Devotional* (Wheaton: Crossway, 2014), 10.

Chapter 2

1 See Rachel Jankovic, *Loving the Little Years: Motherhood in the Trenches* (Moscow, ID: Canon Press, 2010), 40.

Chapter 4

1 Elisabeth Elliot, *Keep a Quiet Heart* (Grand Rapids: Revell, 1995), 20.

Chapter 6

1 Paul David Tripp, *When Suffering Enters Your Door* (Philadelphia, PA: Paul Tripp Ministries, 2013), DVD.

Chapter 8

1 Tripp, *New Morning Mercies*, November 19.

Chapter 9

1 Jennie Allen, *Restless: Because You Were Made for More* (Nashville: W Publishing, 2013), 12.

2 "Westminster Shorter Catechism," *Center for Reformed Theology and Apologetics*, http://www.reformed.org/documents/wsc/index.html?_top =http://www.reformed.org/documents/WSC.html.

3 Brad Bigney, "How Do Idols Get Into My Heart?" *Gospel Treason* video series, https://vimeo.com/album/2287581/video/50531170.

4 Wayne Grudem, *Systematic Theology: An Introduction to Biblical Doctrine* (Leicester, England: Inter-Varsity Press, 1994), 442.

5 Allen, *Restless*, 124.

6 Heather MacFadyen, "Letting Go of Perfect," *God-Centered Mom*

(blog), August 1, 2011, http://godcenteredmom.com/2011/08/01/letting-go-of-perfect/.

Chapter 10

1 Tripp, *New Morning Mercies*, November 9.
2 John Piper, *The Pleasures of God: Meditations on God's Delight in Being God* (Colorado Springs: Multnomah Publishers, 2012), 233.
3 Jason Meyer, "When I Am Weak, then I Am Strong" lecture, Bethlehem Baptist Church, Minneapolis, MN, June 6, 2015, https://www.hopeingod.org/sermon/when-i-am-weak-then-i-am-strong.

Chapter 13

1 Jim Gaffigan, "5 Kids," *Obsessed*, Comedy Central Records, 2014.
2 Brad Bigney, "What Does God Know about My Heart?" *Gospel Treason* video series, https://vimeo.com/album/2287581/video/49605699.
3 Lily Park, "Responding to Emotional Abuse in Marriage," *Biblical Counseling Coalition* (blog), October 1, 2013, http://biblicalcounselingcoalition.org/2013/10/01/responding-to-emotional-abuse-in-marriage/.
4 Lindsey A. Holcomb and Justin S. Holcomb, *Is It My Fault? Hope and Healing for those Suffering Domestic Violence* (Chicago: Moody Press, 2014).

Chapter 14

1 Paul David Tripp, *Instruments in the Redeemer's Hands* (Phillipsburg: P & R Publishing, 2002), 241.
2 John Piper, "How Do You Define Joy?" *Desiring God* (blog), July 25, 2015, http://www.desiringgod.org/articles/how-do-you-define-joy.

About the Author

Maggie Combs is passionate about helping moms recognize their imperfections as opportunities for God's boundless strength. She is the mom of three busy boys: Isaac, Zander, and Judah. She blames their unending energy and solid build completely on her tall, active husband, Wes. Maggie grew up dreaming of motherhood because she assumed it would increase her social life. She thought wrong. Now Maggie uses her stolen moments to write about the down-and-dirty realities of motherhood, occasionally getting these thoughts corralled online on Instagram (@unsupermommy) or unsupermommy.com. She escapes from the crazy by spending quality time with her husband—and her Kindle. Her family is currently building a new house on the hobby farm where she grew up. You can peek into that journey on Instagram by following @bravenewfarmhouse. Maggie would be delighted if you'd reach out to share your own unsupermommy story with her online!

Unsupermommy.com